David Warnock
5/11/18

EXIT TO TOMORROW

exit to tomorrow

WORLD'S FAIR ARCHITECTURE, DESIGN, FASHION **1933–2005**

UNIVERSE ⊛

contents

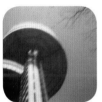

# of imaginary and concrete fantasies

PAOLA ANTONELLI

A GREAT WORLD'S FAIR, JUST LIKE A GOOD SCI-FI MOVIE, is a plausible fantasy based on the impact of science and technology on society. But while the world portrayed by the movies can be on the verge of a dark catastrophe — or just emerging from it — the dream invoked by a world's fair is nearly always a gleaming utopia within arm's reach. Even when it deals with an impending cataclysm (say, our contemporary environmental irresponsibility) or with major disruptions in the world order (from World War I, to the Great Depression, the advent of extremist totalitarian regimes, all the way to World War II), a world's fair does so with a benign smile and an optimistic outlook of salvation. Much like the Berlin Olympic Games of 1936 — conceived to convey a message of world dominance by Adolf Hitler, designed with fanfare by Albert Speer, recorded dramatically by Leni Riefenstahl, and yet usurped by Jesse Owens's four gold medals with a contrasting message of hope and freedom — world's fairs by their own nature were resistant to complete nationalistic manipulation.

Looking for milestones of science-fiction cinematography around the time of this book's inception, we encountered negative visions of progress and technology in the span of nine years, from overtly dark and dirty (Fritz Lang's *Metropolis* of 1927), all the way to deceptively transparent, as in the triumph of glass and polished concrete as the way to enlightened socialism (William Cameron Menzies's *Things to Come* of 1936, written by H. G. Wells and punctuated by László Moholy-Nagy's special effects). It is an almost guilty pleasure to look at the connections between the history of world's fairs and that of bona fide sci-fi entertainment, but even more compelling is to comb the last seventy years of human history for attempts to make these scientific, political, and stylistic dreams come true.

The history of world's fairs is interspersed not only by cinematographic and literary fantasies, but also by real ones. The most arresting is Brasilia, the new South American capital first dreamed by a Catholic saint at the end of the nineteenth century, then dreamed again by a conservative president at the end of the 1950s, and finally built by a team of Communist architects and planners in three years. Lead architect Oscar Niemeyer's Brasilia was an optimistic dream about the future, an ode to the cathartic power of modern architecture. Candid and majestic under the tropical sun, it was built in order to uplift the destinies of Brazil and of the world. Their engineered perfect social integration did not happen. Built as a dream, Brasilia remained a utopia and to this day it looks a bit like an abandoned world's fairground. What makes Niemeyer an architect who is still so relevant and interesting—and also still so controversial, however—is his political habit with beauty, a key aspect of most world's fairs.

The fairs always were experiments of major changes to come. They were Olympic games in which countries competed not with sports, but rather with technology and science, not with muscles and training, but with innovation and imagination. For the first time in history, in the occasion of this pan-games, major industrial manufacturers placed themselves on the same level as countries by building impressive physical and communicative edifices and attracting an equally large and innocently unaware audience—a premonition of the large supra-national corporations of today, which are able to influence international policy as much or even more than individual countries.

Before we knew the power of experiential and interaction design, the fairs promised and delivered. As a matter of fact, the imagination and design of the future is a pursuit that electrifies children and Nobel Prize winners alike, not simply as observers, but rather as active participants. The most powerful examples of architecture ever realized, from the pyramids to the Centre Pompidou, are about much more than their function. They are about emotion and possibility; they are "exits to tomorrow." As architects and designers, we can learn from world's fairs that there is nothing as universal and immediately moving as the feeling of being an active participant in the making of a better world.

Figure 1 Etienne-Louis Boullée, Design for a Cenotaph
for Newton, 1784
Figure 2 Trylon and Perisphere, New York World's Fair,
Flushing Meadows, Queens, 1939/1940
Figure 3 Buckminster Fuller, United States Pavilion,
Expo '67, Montreal, 1967

anticipation of the future: the origin and history of world's fairs

UDO KULTERMANN

1. the formation IN THE EIGHTEENTH CENTURY, the revolutionary approach of Sir Isaac Newton established a basis for standards of scientific evaluation and, at the same time, visions of a globalization for a worldview that earlier could not have been imagined. It transformed ways of thinking since then and continues to do so. In late eighteenth-century architectural projects by Etienne-Louis Boullée, especially in his project Design for a Cenotaph for Newton of 1784 (fig. 1), the new age found a brilliant articulation (fig.2, fig. 3). The historical period was

significantly later; called the "Enlightenment," it metaphorically shed light on dark spaces. Parallel revolutions were established in the writings of Rousseau and Voltaire, and a basic change was followed by the political eruption of the French Revolution. In Kant's philosophy, all these elements created a synthesis that became fundamental for the developments since the nineteenth century. In terms of worldwide opportunities the direction was open for the sequence of architectural transformations, establishing a reality for the globalization and standardization of design on many levels. The desire of countries to participate in a worldwide exchange of their products transformed the earlier local economic systems into a combination of both traditional manufactured goods and newly industrialized products.

These important economic and political transformations took place in the newly established organization of the world's fair, an institution in which various countries could measure their supposed wealth and economic output and compare it with that of other countries. The term "fair" became a modernization of the earlier tradition of the marketplace in which objects became exposed in an international exchange and thus elevated the process to a level of institutional interdependence. One of the surprising results of these opportunities became the freedom of constructions beyond the limitation of earthbound structures and the exploration of previously unknown methods, which only later entered into the mainstream of building. By means of the newly created freedom, the architectural shape of relevant buildings changed the development of architecture in general, anticipating not only circular and elevated designs, but also—later—buildings with extreme dimensions and flexible, mobile, and inflatable features. The history of world's fairs thus is a demonstration of building structures in which future developments were articulated, anticipating innovative changes in general.

The roots of these new developments lay in France and England: in France the institution of Industrial Fairs gave inspiration to new possibilities; and in England globalization was a reality, including handcrafted products from the colonial territories and industrial products from the factories. World's fairs opened a new historic period in which exchange of products from all parts of the world played a new and differently evaluated role. The building type of exhibiting this multiplicity of goods served a new function and, in addition, had creative, innovative impacts on other building types as well.

2. the miracle of 1851

Major buildings designed and built for world's fairs have since become historically significant to architectural development in spite of their temporary existence, for example, the two major buildings of the Paris World's Fair of 1889: the Eiffel Tower and the Hall of Machines. Other still-existing structures designed and built for world's fairs are the Grand Palais by Henri Doglane and the Petit Palais by Charles Louis Girault, both in Paris; the Habitat '67 in Montreal by Moshe Safdie; and the Atomium in Brussels of 1958 by Andre and Jean Polak and Andre Waterkeyn. Future insights, historic reevaluations, and additional cultural implications of world's fairs of the past remain open.

There is one building in which the new developments are clearly manifested, and the elements of world economy, political ambitions, and the innovations of industrialization and mass production are combined: the Crystal Palace in London of 1851 (fig. 4). Its importance became evident in the mutual efforts made by Henry Cole, the director of London's Royal Society of Arts, and supported by Prince Albert and the engineers Isambard Kingdom Brunel, Joseph Paxton, and George and Robert Stephenson. After visiting the Industrial Exhibition in Paris in 1848 Cole arranged a similar show within the Royal Society of Arts in which the innovative international tendencies were evident. Brunel became instrumental with his suggestion of a national competition in 1850 for the first world's fair, in which 233 architects participated. The timing was unrealistic: the anticipated opening of the world's fair in May 1851 would not allow enough time to wait for the results of the competition and construct traditional types of buildings. A completely new material and construction process was needed, one that would incorporate the prefabrication of industrial elements and their transportation by rail. Beyond technology, the new potential of mass communication played a part in the promotion and final result of the project. In the *Illustrated London News* of June 6, 1850, a design, obviously inspired by Brunel, was published. Paxton sent his own design on July 6, 1850, to Mr. Ellis, a member of Parliament who supported

Figure 4 Joseph Paxton, Crystal Palace, London, 1851

Paxton's plan. Paxton's collaboration with George and Robert Stephenson finally received support from Buckingham Palace. Some days later, on July 16, 1850, the officially appointed commission supported the design, now in collaboration with the firm Fox and Henderson. The project was conceived in prefabricated elements of wood, glass, and iron and included a transept with a wooden barrel vault.

The work began at sensational speed, and in about six months it was completed. The total length of the Crystal Palace was 1,851 feet (564 meters) to symbolize the year of the structure. The central nave was twenty-two meters high and intersected by a transept of twenty-two meters. The plan was dominated by a module of seven meters. In spite of the sensational new design there were also historical references observed by contemporaries. The basic structure was a type of basilica in the tradition of early Christian basilicas in Rome, a fact that was recognized and praised by Lady Carlisle, who compared the building with St. Peter's.

The unique character of the building and the shortness of time in which it was designed and erected was furthermore significant, as it prefigured the work of twentieth-century designers. The total structure was conceived in a proportional module, and according to the concepts of Owen Jones, in the primary colors of red, blue, and yellow. Still another innovative and revolutionary element was the inclusion of the large elm trees in Hyde Park as part of the interior space. Anticipating much later building principles, the new project by Paxton actually became a "turning point in architecture" as Konrad Wachsmann much later defined it.

As with the Eiffel Tower in Paris three decades later, vehement opposition arose in London against the new building in Hyde Park, especially with concern for the safety of the structure, which was questioned due to the new and unknown construction technique. Many opponents argued that mathematicians had calculated that the Crystal Palace would blow down in the first strong gale; engineers said the galleries would crack and destroy the visitors. The concept and realization of the 1851 World's Fair, as with many later world's fairs, was a heavily debated struggle.

Nevertheless, the completed building and its international success remained the focal point of a continued philosophical debate between major writers of the time, among them John Ruskin and William Morris. For Ruskin and his violent attacks against the domination of machine technology, the Crystal Palace was nothing more than a "cucumber nursery." One of the most positive appraisals was an entry in the diary of the young Queen Victoria describing the opening ceremonies on May 1, 1851, as a "Peace-Festival": "The immensity of the building, the mixture of palms, flowers, fountains, and my beloved husband as the author of this 'Peace-Festival' which united the industry of the earth." But, part of the "symbol of peace" in 1851 was the first presentation of the Krupp Canons, which were included in this and later world's fairs with special promotion and financial help by the German government. There were also products of the French weapons industry, and the American contribution to the 1851 fair included revolvers by Cyrus McCormick and Samuel Colt. A controversial image of the peace-oriented ideology of the world's fairs was *The Angel of Peace* at the fair of 1862, which showed the figure of an angel sitting on a gun. Another landmark of the tendency toward globalization was the Great Globe exhibited at the 1851 fair, symbolizing its worldwide ambitions. The globe would be seen in several variations at later fairs, among them in an enlarged version at the center of the fair in 1964 New York, where it still stands today.

The international success and economic impact of the 1851 fair was important: 13,937 exhibitors from England and the English Dominions participated, as well as 6,556 foreign exhibitors. The number of objects exhibited transcended one hundred thousand on an area of 92,146 square meters, and more than six million visitors attended, creating a profit of £186,437 for the organizers. The fair lasted from May 1 to October 11. The series of images of the fair by George Cruikshank, "Visit to the Great Exhibition of 1851," depicted the event as a worldwide attraction and opened a discussion on reusing it for different purposes. An enlarged version of the Crystal Place with two additional vaulted transepts was built between 1852 and 1854 in Sydenham and was successful until it was destroyed by fire in 1939.

Following the closing of the Crystal Palace in 1854, a philosophical debate about its meaning emerged. After a trip to London and a visit to the Crystal Palace, the Russian writer N. Chernyshevsky defined it in his book *What Is To Be Done* of 1863 as a symbol for a utopian socialist society: "For everyone there will be eternal spring and joy everlasting." Another Russian writer, Fyodor Dostoyevsky, created a counterimage of the Crystal Palace, referring back to Voltaire's critical questioning of utopian thinking concepts under the term "molehill." Dostoyevsky concluded accordingly: "I don't accept as the crowning of my dreams a big building for the poor, with apartments leased for one thousand years and a dentist sign outside in case of emergency." The pioneering technology of the first world's fair was programmatically questioned by Dostoyevsky and accused to be nothing else "but a big swindle."

3. worldwide expansion, 1851–89

There was no doubt that the first World's Fair building in London and its controversy had an enormous impact on world's fairs as a new institution and on architecture in general. The fairs in Dublin and Munich were both named Crystal Palaces, as was the structure in the New York's fair of 1853, which was definitely modeled after Paxton's design. The World's Fair in New York, designed by the architects Carstensen and Gildemeister, was located at the corner of Fifth Avenue and Forty-second Street and, as in the Crystal Palace in London, all exhibits were contained under one roof, but without the strong support of the government. The building in New York had many shortcomings and burnt down in 1858.

An unexecuted design for the New York fair (fig. 5) was produced by the architect James Bogardus in the shape of an amphitheater with a diameter of 365 meters and a central tower with an elevator, one of the earliest adaptations of this new invention in large scale. The material in the design was cast iron, which was supposed to be reused for new purposes after the fair. The most innovative element of the project was the cable net that was to cover the circular space between the central tower and the circular amphitheatric building.

The required space for most of the subsequent fair buildings became insufficient, and exhibits could no longer be under only one roof, thus requiring a number of pavilions. There were many world's fairs between 1854 and 1889. Some of them commemorated specific historic events, such as the Centennial Fair in Philadelphia of 1876 with the chief designer H. J. Schwarzmann, who built the Horticultural Hall as the center of the fair. A specific attraction was the right arm and torch of the still incomplete Statue of Liberty (fig. 6), also called the "Electric Light" or "The Statue of Independence," which was first presented to the American public at the 1876 fair.

Figure 5 James Bogardus, Unexecuted Design for the New York World's Fair, 1853

The French sculptor Bartholdi and his American supporters believed that the symbol of the torch as the expression of liberty would kindle the American interest in the work, which was unveiled ten years later in New York Harbor. Light, peace, and freedom were seen and interpreted in harmony: the statue was thus lighting the world.

The inner construction of the Statue of Liberty was designed by Gustave Eiffel (1832–1923), who in the same year also developed a curvilinear building in Paris for the World's Fair. Under the direction of the engineer J. B. S. Krantz, the compartments of this structure were divided into sectional fragments, and the overall scheme resembled the world in its curved oval. In the center was a sculpture garden that gave access to the compartments of the different nations. The planning was by Frederic Le Play (1806–1870). The overall scheme of the structure was included in a painting by Edouard Manet.

Figure 6 Right arm and torch of the Statue of Liberty, Centennial Fair, Philadelphia, 1876

The international success of the Paris fair was illustrated by an increase from seventeen thousand exhibitors in London of 1851 to sixty thousand in Paris in 1867, with an attendance of 6.8 million visitors. The number in attendance at the Paris fair of 1889 rose to 28,121,975, and reached a culmination in the St. Louis fair of 1904 with about fifty million. Other world's fairs with high attendances took place in Vienna in 1873, Sydney and Melbourne in 1879, and Antwerp in 1885.

Figure 7 Gustave Eiffel, Eiffel Tower, World's Fair, Paris, 1889
Figure 8 Hall of Machines, World's Fair, Paris, 1889

4. culmination, 1894–04

The increased worldwide significance of world's fairs was that they not only incorporated products of Western countries, such as industrialization, electrical light, and new means of communication, but also historic elements from non-Western civilizations. Examples of this were the Japanese Bazaar in the Philadelphia fair of 1876 and the reconstruction of Angkor Wat in the Paris Exhibition of 1889, as well as Japanese structures at the Chicago fair of 1893. It is significant that elements of preindustrial periods were seen as valuable contributions.

The Paris fair of 1889 culminated in two buildings that highlighted the developments to come, one being the Eiffel Tower at the center of the exhibition (fig. 7), the other the Hall of Machines (fig. 8) with a space concept that had never been attempted. The engineers Contamin and Dutert created a structure of unprecedented space: a width of 105 meters, a height of 55 meters, and a length of 420 meters. Whereas Paxton's design for the Crystal Palace was achieved by elements of individual cells, here a space was given a new dynamic order with previously unknown dimensions. Beyond the pioneering achievements of Paxton's Crystal Palace, the innovative use of new material was achieved. Additional elements were the movable platforms that carried roughly one hundred thousand visitors throughout the enormous space. The new mobility of the age was brilliantly demonstrated in the new space concept with the capability to integrate these achievements into a new worldview. Henri Adams was extremely fascinated by the hall when he visited it in 1900 and admired the exhibited steam engine and the dynamo, which for him carried nearly mystical sensations. Unfortunately, the Hall of Machines was demolished in 1910.

The second sensational structure in Paris in the fair of 1889 was designed to commemorate the anniversary of the French Revolution of 1789, making the fair a symbol of historical significance. In 1884 plans were made for projects to symbolize this event. Among the entries were a gigantic guillotine and figurative designs of a giant water pitcher and a mirror. As in Paxton's design, all competing entries in the Paris competition were in favor of Eiffel's revolutionary design for a 300-meter tower that became the center of the fair and of the city of Paris. (There was one earlier proposal by Sebillot for a stone tower by means of which the city of Paris would be illuminated, demonstrating again the significance and meaning of electricity, which was officially introduced in the fair of 1878.) The Eiffel Tower would transcend the then highest monuments in history, the Ulm Münster and the obelisk in Washington, D.C., by more than doubling their size.

Work began on January 28, 1887, with Eiffel's collaborators, Naugier and Sauvestre, who designed the four masonry bases, which were then combined to make one enormous tower. Every part was produced in the factory, then numbered and detailed with millions of holes before finding their proper place in the overall design. Eiffel devoted his energy to the completion of the work, which was from the beginning rejected by writers, artists, and architects who protested "in the name of French taste and in the spirit of national culture" against the erection of this monstrosity of a tower. In addition, it was argued that a mathematician had predicted that the building would collapse beyond the height of 228 meters, as "scientists" had also predicted, for other reasons, would happen to Paxton's Crystal Palace. In spite of these warnings, work continued, and in 1888 the first part of the tower reached the platform where the restaurant would be constructed. On May 15, 1888, the second platform was reached, and in December 1888 the opening ceremony of the World's Fair took place. Gustave Eiffel walked up the 1,710 steps, as the elevator was not yet completed.

The building became a symbol of France and of Paris, in spite of the many critical views that still prevailed. In his book *Certains*, J. K. Huysmans saw the structure as a framework waiting to be filled with bricks and blocks. He saw skeletal structures as unacceptable for contemporary works of architecture. It was the work by an engineer in which the necessary changes of structure and volume were first manifested in a spectacular building. The Eiffel Tower has remained in its place as a new idea of a building, the first monumental example of the skeleton building technique that makes no distinction between exterior and interior space. It demonstrated the extreme possibilities of new material and opened up dimensions for building in the future. The originally existing historical ornaments of the tower were partly removed in 1937 in an attempt to conform to the newly developed criteria of "modernity."

It is also significant that Eiffel worked, ahead of his time, on pioneering experiments with flying machines in his laboratory on top of the tower. In 1907 Eiffel's results were published in his book *Recherche expérimentale* and his experiments resulted in realistic types of airplanes known as Breguet LE. The Eiffel Tower became a bridge between the achievements of the experimenting engineer and the new airplane technology.

The fairs in Chicago of 1893 and 1900 and in St. Louis of 1904 shared an awareness of historical reference: the discovery of America by Columbus and the exploration of the territory of the states west of the Mississippi. For example, the 1893 Chicago fair (Columbian Exposition) marked a change of direction by replacing the dominance on technology with historic references to French models. After many years of planning under the guidance of John Wellborn Root, Chicago offered an urbanistic scheme in which the American Middle West was in harmony with the European traditions. Root died in 1891, thus leaving a large part of the planning to his collaborator, Daniel H. Burnham (1846–1912), who changed the general attitude toward a more classicist outlook. Burnham selected five prominent Amer-

Figure 9 Louis Sullivan, Transportation Building, Columbian Exposition, Chicago, 1893
Figure 10 E. Coignet, Palace of Electricity, World's Fair, Paris, 1900

Figure 11 Cliff Dwellings, World's Fair, St. Louis, 1904

ican firms for the main buildings of the fair: R. M. Hunt for the Administration Building; Robert Swain Peabody and John Goddard Sterns for the Hall of Machines; McKim, Mead and White for the Agricultural Building; Henry Van Brunt and Frank Maynard Brunt for the Electrical Hall; and George Browne Post for the Manufacturers and Liberal Arts Building. All of the designs were historically and predominantly French in character and built in temporary material, which was painted white, thus the fair was called the "White City." With the ambition of symbolizing eternity, but in their realization very transient, all the buildings were demolished after the end of the fair.

Representing the non-Western parts of the world at the Chicago fair were the Samoan Village, also called the South Sea Islands Village, and the Arabian Village, in which people from these areas were made part of the exhibition. Also fundamental was the contribution by Frederick Law Olmsted, who included gardens and waterways in the 633-acre fairground. The Chicago fair included movable sidewalks on the Casino Pier, which for ten cents gave visitors the opportunity to overview the entire fair. Other attractions were the Giant Ferris Wheels, invented by George Ferris, and the Krupp Canon, which was transported by the Krupp Gun Company in Essen, Germany, at a cost of $500,000. The canon was donated after the fair to the city of Chicago. The twenty-seven million visitors made the fair one of the most popular events of the decade.

The major buildings by Richard M. Hunt and Henry Ives Cobb continued the classical French domination in spite of such innovative structures as the Transportation Building by Louis Sullivan (fig. 9) and the Women's Building by Sophia Hayden. Nevertheless, some of the revolutionary architects, namely Frank Lloyd Wright, saw the fair as a setback to America's architectural development.

The Paris 1900 fair incorporated earlier technological achievements, including the Eiffel Tower, the Hall of Machines, and other important engineering structures, often with historical ornamentation. The two buildings of the fair that still stand today are the Grand Palais by Henri Deglane and the Petit Palais by Charles Louis Girault, both encompassing the tradition of French historical decoration.

The international success of the fair culminated in the attendance of more than forty-eight million. The highly ornamented Palace of Electricity by E. Coignet (fig. 10) was a spectacular pavilion that gave the new medium of electric light a dominating role. A smaller building by the architect Henri Sauvage was conceived for the American dancer Loie Fuller, who performed using electric light and veils. The Finnish Pavilion was an early art nouveau work by Eliel Saarinen. The movable walkways were once again used throughout the fair and were much later reintroduced at the fair in Osaka, Japan. Of historic significance were the stations of the Paris Metro, which were designed by Hector Guimard and completed for the opening of the fair.

The 1904 World's Fair in St. Louis, Missouri, attempted to compete with the earlier events in Chicago and Paris. It took on special significance by integrating both the Olympic Games and the World's Fair at the same time. The existing St. Louis Art Museum by Cass Gilbert, in its dominating position on a hill in Forest Park, was originally conceived as a Festival Hall. This building, as well as the various national pavilions, created a panoramic ensemble in which entertainment facilities played an important role. The most radical incorporation of non-Western culture was manifested in the famous Cliff Dwellings: not only were the housing patterns of Native Americans part of the exhibition, but the inhabitants themselves were brought to the fair in order to give an authentic view of their lifestyle (fig. 11). Their dwellings, composed of mud-brick building material, greatly influenced the young generation of American architects, especially Frank Lloyd Wright, who later developed comparable forms of residential architecture in his houses in California.

5. private corporate power and state power: the 1930s

The sequence of international fairs came to a halt with the onset of World War I and the subsequent political transformation in Russia, Italy, and Germany. The American development of world's fairs was dominated by the pavilions of large corporations, predominantly the automobile companies. In Europe a small number of creative architects became part of the revolutionary architectural development with buildings that didn't compete in size with the major pavilions of earlier fairs. One of these buildings was the Pavilion de L'Esprit Nouveau by Le Corbusier of 1925, and another was the Pavilion of the Soviet Union by the architect Konstantin Melnikov, both in Paris and both articulating a different version of the new architectural possibilities. The third building was the German Pavilion in the World's Fair in Barcelona in 1929 by Ludwig Mies van der Rohe (fig. 13). All three buildings were masterpieces of architecture in general. Mies's pavilion in Barcelona was a brilliant spatial environment in which the harmonious proportions and selective materials constituted a concept of architectural refinement. Werner Hofmann described the special achievement of the pavilion as the abolishment of the borders between the interior and the exterior space: "The main and subsidiary pavilions were open in several directions, and rhythmically connected by an articulating wall." Hofmann justly concluded this as an "interpenetration" of an organic space concept, exploring possibilities that did not require objects for an exhibition.

Figure 13 Ludwig Mies van der Rohe, German Pavilion, World's Fair, Barcelona, 1929
© Berliner Bild-Bericht / Fundació Mies van der Rohe-Barcelona

The Great Depression, both in America and Europe, reduced architectural activities, but nevertheless created ambitious programs to promote optimistic visions of the future. The potential of industrial and economic prospects often were in the center, and terms such as "Progress" and "Futurama" were often propagated.

The major center of the fairs in Chicago of 1933/1934 and later in New York of 1939 were large-scale environmental structures that culminated in the "A Century of Progress" exhibition in Chicago. The architect Albert Kahn (1896–1942) worked for both Ford and General Motors, as well as the Chrysler Corporation. He introduced a modernist language in industrial architecture and design, which adapted by means of production from the earlier methods into efficient ways of use for the assembly line. Anticipation of the future was seen as one of the major topics of the Chicago fair and was defined in slogans such as "The Century of Progress" and "The World of Tomorrow." The designer Joseph Urban (1872–1933) contributed to these themes and also excelled with various unexecuted projects. The New York architect Raymond Hood was commissioned to build a group of Electrical Buildings that represented the spirit of the time. One of the most prominent buildings in Chicago and in the "A Century of Progress" exhibition was the Italian Pavilion by Adalberto Libera, Mario De Renzi, Antonio Valente, and

IN THE EIGHTEENTH CENTURY, the revolutionary approach of Sir Isaac Newton established a basis for standards of scientific evaluation and, at the same time, visions of a globalization for a worldview that earlier could not have been imagined. It transformed ways of thinking since then and continues to do so. In late eighteenth-century architectural projects by Etienne-Louis Boullée, especially in his project Design for a Cenotaph for Newton of 1784 (fig. 1), the new age found a brilliant articulation (fig.2, fig. 3). The historical period was significantly later; called the "Enlightenment," it metaphorically shed light on dark spaces. Parallel revolutions were established in the writings of Rousseau and Voltaire, and a basic change was followed by the political eruption of the French Revolution. In Kant's philosophy, all these elements created a synthesis that became fundamental for the developments since the nineteenth century. In terms of worldwide opportunities the direction was open for the sequence of architectural transformations, establishing a reality for the globalization and standardization of design on many levels. The desire of countries to participate in a worldwide exchange of their products transformed the earlier local economic systems into a combination of both traditional manufactured goods and newly industrialized products.

These important economic and political transformations took place in the newly established organization of the world's fair, an institution in which various countries could measure their supposed wealth and economic output and compare it with that of other countries. The term "fair" became a modernization of the earlier tradition of the marketplace in which objects became exposed in an international exchange and thus elevated the process to a level of institutional interdependence. One of the surprising results of these opportunities became the freedom of constructions beyond the limitation of earthbound structures and the exploration of previously unknown methods, which only later entered into the mainstream of building. By means of the newly created freedom, the architectural shape of relevant buildings changed the development of architecture in general, anticipating not only circular and elevated designs, but also—later—buildings with extreme dimensions and flexible, mobile, and inflatable features. The history of world's fairs thus is a demonstration of building structures in which future developments were articulated, anticipating innovative changes in general.

The roots of these new developments lay in France and England: in France the institution of Industrial Fairs gave inspiration to new possibilities; and in England globalization was a reality, including handcrafted products from the colonial territories and industrial products from the factories. World's fairs opened a new historic period in which exchange of products from all parts of the world played a new and differently evaluated role. The building type of exhibiting this multiplicity of goods served a new function and, in

Figure 14 Sky Ride, A Century of Progress Exposition, Chicago, 1933/1934
Figure 15 Trylon and Perisphere, New York World's Fair, Flushing Meadows, Queens, 1939/1940

Figure 16 Esposizione Universale di Roma (EUR), Rome, 1942

Speer—were positioned in an aggressive confrontation. Both were in the center of the fairground, and in their architectural language openly confronted each other, demonstrating the reality of the political situation in Europe at the time. In both buildings the sculptural language was furthermore emphasized in the statue by Vera Mukhina in the Soviet Pavilion and in the sculpture by Arno Breker in the German Pavilion. A clear anticipation of the political and militarist events to follow a few years later was evident. The counter movement was the inclusion of Picasso's *Guernica*, which was exhibited in the Spanish Pavilion built by José Luis Sert. For the first time, a non-Western country was part of the fair: the Japanese Pavilion was designed by the architect Junzo Sakakura, who at that time was working in the Paris office of Le Corbusier. It was a genuine demonstration of a contemporary form of international architecture by a Japanese architect. A special visitors' attraction was the illumination of the Eiffel Tower, given the name "Parachute Tower."

Political development was increased by the attempts to create a new grand capital of Italy, southwest of Rome, with the 1942 world's fair, called the Esposizione Universale di Roma or EUR (fig. 16). The planning and design was conceived on an urbanistic scale from the beginning. Supported by Mussolini in early 1936, it was designed by two teams of Italian architects, one under the directorship of Marcelo Piacentini, the other team by Giuseppe Pagano. Both aimed at an urbanistic articulation of the new capital of Rome outside the limits of the city. Among the parts completed was the Palazzo della Civiltà del Lavoro by the architects Giovanni Guer- rini, Ernesto La Padula, and Marco Romano, with its 216 round arches containing partially finished statues. The most impressive designs of the fair were arches by Adalberto Libera and Cesare Pascoletti, which, like many other structures, remained unbuilt.

The most important building in the Rome fair was the Palazzo del Congressi by Adalberto Libera, which was completed in 1955 and would have been the background for the main ceremonies of the fair. According to the design, the building's dimensions were thirty-six by thirty-six by thirty-sixmeters, matching those of the Roman Pantheon. Libera was attempting to create a contemporary equivalent to "a Pantheon in Reinforced Concrete." Interconnections between the past and present were envisioned in gigantic arches by Pascoletti and Libera but never built.

Figure 17 Egon Eiermann, German Pavilion, Expo '58, Brussels, 1958
Figure 18 Karl Schwanzer, Austrian Pavilion, Expo '58, Brussels, 1958
Figure 19 Le Corbusier, Philips Pavilion, Expo '58, Brussels, 1958

6. postwar new beginnings (Brussels, New York, Montreal and Osaka)

The development of world's fairs after World War II took on a new direction beyond the dictatorial and commercial demonstrations before the war. An exchange of international trade and culture was manifested in large-scale collaborations. In the Brussels fair of 1958, countries participated with individual pavilions that surrounded the newly introduced dominating symbol of the Atomium, seen as a sign for the new age of the peaceful use of nuclear energy. Designed by Andre and Jean Polak and Andre Waterkeyn, it consisted of a sequence of large metal circular spheres elevated from the ground and interconnected by moving stairways, creating a dynamic ensemble in the air. The 110-meter structure, built in the form of an atom 165 billion times enlarged, was taller than the nationalistic symbols of the U.S. and Soviet Pavilions, both of which had a strong presence in shaping the environment of the fair. Unlike the monumental pavilion in Paris, the German Pavilion in Brussels by Egon Eiermann (fig. 17) was reduced to a modest sequence of horizontal spaces. Other national pavilions, such as those for Norway by Sverre Fehn and Finland by Reima Pietilae, became exemplary for the tradition of their respective countries by concentrating on the use of wood as material. The Austrian Pavilion by Karl Schwanzer (fig. 18) was re-erected after the fair as the Museum of 20th Century Art in Vienna, and the pavilion of Czechoslovakia by the architects Cubr, Hruby and Pokorny, designed as a restaurant

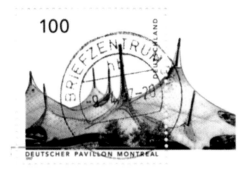

DEUTSCHER PAVILLON MONTREAL

Figure 20 Frei Otto, German Pavilion, Expo '67, Montreal, 1967
Figure 21 Moshe Safdie, Habitat '67, Expo '67, Montreal, 1967

with open terraces, was rebuilt in Prague after the end of the fair.

Of special significance was the Philips Pavilion by Le Corbusier (fig. 19), in which an innovative combination of music and electronic projection was achieved by expanding the thematics of space, color, and sound, including contemporary composers, as well as the participation of the user. The curvilinear shape opened up new possibilities of design and had wide-reaching impacts on architecture in general.

Following Brussels was the World's Fair in New York, which opened on April 22, 1964. Dominated by the large pavilions of the American corporations—among them General Motors, Kodak, and Chrysler—it continued the tradition of the earlier Chicago and New York fairs. As a motto it chose the theme "Peace through Understanding," referring to the early concept of Queen Victoria of 1851. In the center of the fair in Flushing, Queens, the New York State Pavilion by Philip Johnson and Norman Foster was an open structure that could be used for a variety of public events. It was decorated with large-scale works by artists, among them, Rauschenberg, Lichtenstein, Warhol, and Rosenquist—the dominating artists of the emerging pop art style. The mural by Warhol was painted over in one day on orders from Robert Moses. A significant symbol of the world was the stainless steel Unisphere, which is reminiscent of the globe in the first World's Fair of 1851 in London.

The World's Fair in Montreal of 1967

expanded the earlier developments by transcending the previous limitations of the fairs in Central Europe and America. It also expanded technological innovations with the inclusion of a residential quarter for permanent use. The central pavilions were devoted to the U.S. and Soviet Union, both asserting their political and technological dominance. Fuller's spectacular dome was one of the major attractions. Following the earlier developments of his geodesic domes, Fuller created knot joints linking the outside net of thick struts, which carries most of the weight, with the inner set, on which two thousand acrylic painted caps were mounted. Motors at the joints reacted automatically to the sunlight, moving a system of sun blinds and a number of hexagonal caps containing a ventilation system. The pavilion, described by Fuller as a "geodesic skyscraper dome," had a spherical diameter of about 250 feet and a maximum height of 200 feet. The surface measured 14,000 square feet. Under the shell, through which the exhibition monorail ran, the exhibition floors were arranged independently on several levels joined by elevators. Fuller's concept allowed parts to be replaced.

The German Pavilion in Montreal by Frei Otto (fig. 20) opened new constructive possibilities. It consisted of a cable net suspended from eight tubular steel masts under which was a stretched polyester skin. This covered an exhibition space made out of steel-frame parts and arranged in terraces forming two spirals. There was also an auditorium with two galleries covered by a shell made up of wooden slats. All parts of the structure were extremely cheap and made in Germany, then individually packed and shipped to Montreal where every part was assembled. The cost of the building was extremely low, remaining under the estimated budget.

Of great importance for the fair in Montreal and the developments of world's fairs in general was the residential unit of Habitat '67, commissioned to the young Israeli architect Moshe Safdie (fig. 21). It was originally scheduled to contain one thousand units, but due to lack of money only 160 were built. The prefabricated units were arranged into twelve pyramidal shaped stories. The ensemble resulted in an elevated environment of prefabricated boxes, which were fixed together in varying shapes. Each unit was about thirty-seven feet long, nineteen feet wide, and eleven feet high, and weighed ninety tons. The individual units were prefabricated on site, sandblasted, and equipped with walls, floors, services, and kitchens and then lifted into place by a crane. There were three different sizes: the smallest was a single block; larger apartments could be of three or four units. Every apartment had a balcony formed by the roof of the box below. Prefabrication was once again fundamental as it was in Paxton's Crystal Palace in London in 1851, only here utilizing a different material for a permanent residential unit.

When in 1965 Osaka was selected for the World's Fair of 1970, a new phase was initiated, especially when Kenzo Tange was commissioned to design the project. Tange invited twelve architects who had worked for him before, among them Kiyonori Kikutake, Kisho Kurokawa, Arata Isozaki, and Masato Otaka to contribute individual works. For Tange a new concept for Expo '70 was crucial. His idea as an urbanist was for software rather than the earlier hardware solutions in previous world's fairs. The Festival Plaza, which dominated the complete design, included an artificial lake. The individual pavilions determined the locations of the overall scheme, which Tange conceived as a tree with branches defined as fruits, leaves, or flowers. An anticipated fifty million visitors would experience a pedestrian walking system, as first introduced in the Paris fair of 1878 and the fair in New York of 1900, as well as a vertically moving restaurant by Kurokawa, which allowed for a permanently changing overview of the totality of the exhibition.

The dynamic structure of the pavilion of the Soviet Union was designed by Mikhail Posokhin (fig. 22) and celebrated the revolutionary achievements of Soviet space technology. Other important pavilions were the Beautillion and the Toshiba IHI Pavilion by Kisho Kurokawa, the latter conceived as a rotating circular auditorium. Yutaka Murata and M. Kawaguchi conceived the Fuji Pavilion as a pneumatic structure created by the differences of air pressure in the various elements. The American Pavilion designed by Lewis Davis and Samuel Brody was an oval-shaped space covered with a large space-frame roof.

Figure 22 Mikhail Posokhin, Soviet Union Pavilion, Expo '70, Osaka, 1970

7. contemporary perspectives

Figure 23 Tadao Ando, Japanese Pavilion, Seville, 1992

The development of world's fairs in the last decade showed a shift from earlier concepts to new possibilities. For example, major nations and large corporations built less imposing manifestations. Technology continued to be in the process of transformation, and new interrelations between micro and macro scale objectives remain, as do the incorporation of laser and electronic devices. The new emphasis shows the potential for an attitude that is only in its beginnings.

In comparison with the large-scale realizations at the world's fairs in Montreal and Osaka, the shift toward less ambitious and less monumental results is evident, articulating the different economic realities. The strong overall domination of urbanistic and comprehensive designs has been replaced with more individual and formal images in which the identity of the country is visible. The use of wood as the dominating material in pavilions of Japan and the Scandinavian countries is already anticipated. Thus features of industrial globalization have been reduced, and more regional-oriented solutions are being introduced.

The fairs in Seville, Hannover, and Aichi demonstrate examples in the new direction. Tadao Ando's 1992 Japanese Pavilion in Seville (fig. 23) is a prime example. The four-storied pavilion is one of the largest wooden buildings in the world and represents a change in Ando's work from his frequent use of reinforced concrete. When Ando was given the prestigious Pritzker Prize in 1995, the architect characterized this building as a bridge from the Occident to the Orient. For the fair in Seville the Spanish engineer Santiago Calatrava was commissioned to build the pavilion for Kuwait, a country that was never before represented in a worldwide context. By means of the flexibility of the roof structure with elements that opened and closed, a new climatic condition was achieved.

In the Japanese Pavilion at the 2000 fair in Hannover, the Japanese architect Shigeru Ban went even further by choosing inexpensive found building materials and using them in a method of unorthodox flexibility. The same materials could be used again for different projects. Cardboard tubes were used again in the Japanese Pavilion at Aichi in 2005.

It is significant that the major contributions in recent fairs were provided not by famous, established architects and engineers, but by those—as in the past—who explored the possibilities of a future direction. Thus architects and engineers such as Tadao Ando, Santiago Calatrava (fig. 24), and Shigeru Ban belong to the tradition of pioneers such as Joseph Paxton, Gustave Eiffel, Buckminster Fuller, and Frei Otto from the earlier history of world's fairs.

In his *Historic Observations of 1827* Victor Hugo envisioned the essence of history and culture of the world as a dynamic and changing reality, one that would not be static or restricted to a region of the world. For Hugo civilization began at a distinct location and moved according to the changing systems of power to another center, always remaining on the move, according to the changes in reality. For Hugo this was specifically a shift from authority to freedom. Social progress was an optimistic view that was not only manifested in political and social development but also visible in the building tasks of world's fairs. World's fairs were thus determined according to the specific economical and technological conditions in which they could happen. In this sense it was not by chance that the city of London had the necessary conditions to initiate such an event. Later fairs expanded to other parts of the world under conditions also right for the time, such as cities in America like New York, Chicago, Philadelphia, and St. Louis.

World's fairs defined the general developments of events and technological progress as well as the interconnections between countries. In this process they contributed a number of extraordinary and exciting buildings that incorporated the hope of selected architects and engineers to define the shape of their dreams of the future and to anticipate the direction of the coming developments.

Figure 24 Santiago Calatrava, Kuwait Pavilion, World's Fair, Seville, 1992

CHICAGO

1933/1934

IN 1933, ON THE SAME SITE AS THE 1893 COLUMBIAN EXPOSITION, Chicago welcomed exhibits and visitors from around the world. Called "A Century of Progress," this exposition commemorated the one hundredth anniversary of the incorporation of the city. Planned at the beginning of the Great Depression, the fair was planned to boost Chicago's economy and the morale of its citizens. It proved so profitable and popular that organizers decided the fair, originally scheduled for just six months, should reopen the following year. Indeed, the success of "A Century of Progress" in bolstering the economy prompted other cities to approach world's fairs as economic generators.

The fair opened with a grand publicity stunt when the lights were supposedly turned on by the energy from the star Arcturus. The star was chosen because it was exactly forty light years away from Earth, and thus its light had theoretically began its journey to Earth at the time of Chicago's previous world's fair in 1893. In *The Official Pictures of A Century of Progress Exposition*, James Weber Linn writes, "That the lights of A Century of Progress should have been turned on by the impulse of the very rays which were darting from the star Arcturus when the old World's Fair was in progress forty years ago, is strikingly characteristic…. No man or woman present on the first occasion, or on any subsequent occasion indeed, when 'Arcturus turned on the lights,' is likely to forget it, or to deny that poetry and drama are allied to scientific thought and deed, that imagination is hidden in the very heart of science."

Every aspect of the fair was crafted to provoke wonder and excitement among the visitors. Among the exhibits, there was a "midget village" featuring sixty "Lilliputians," babies in incubators, and a Hollywood display with a live sound stage and 3-D movies. In October 1933, the German airship Graf Zeppelin arrived at the fair and floated over Lake Michigan. The Sky Ride, the symbol of the fair, carried passengers across the fairgrounds on a transporter bridge perpendicular to Lake Michigan's shore. Designed by Robinson and Steinman, the Sky Ride was 628 feet high and spanned 1,850 feet. During the second year of the fair, the organizers sought to distinguish this fair from the infamous "White City" of the Columbian Exposition. They appointed a director of color, Joseph Urban, to develop a deeply saturated color scheme. All the fair designers worked within this color set, including chief designer Louis Skidmore of Skidmore, Owings & Merrill. This "Rainbow City," as it was called, had a palette of twenty-three colors and was illuminated by white and colored lights at night.

The "Homes of Tomorrow" exhibit promoted new construction techniques, innovative building materials, and the conveniences promised by modern technology. The House of Tomorrow, designed by Keck & Keck, was a ten-sided, three-story steel-framed home, clad in glass. It included an early television, and garages complete with a Dymaxion car and a Pratt-Whitney personal airplane. Other model homes featured modular metal construction, electronically controlled doors, and recirculating air and air conditioning.

With its blend of romanticism, entertainment, and optimism about the future, the "A Century of Progress" fair proved to be wildly popular with the public and financially successful for its organizers. It became an oft-cited model of how an exposition could stimulate the economy and generate innovative design and technologies.

previous spread
The Chrysler Motors Building, designed by Holabird & Root, showcased the latest Dodge, Plymouth, and Chrysler cars. The building's tall vertical shafts and large display windows evoked the streamlined aesthetics of the automobiles of the day.

opposite
In the Travel and Transport Building, designers John A. Holabird, Edward J. Bennett, and Hubert Burnham employed the principles of the suspension bridge to construct the dome. No pillars, columns, or arches were necessary. At the time, the dome was the largest unobstructed area under one roof in the world.

left
The June 3, 1933, cover of World's Fair Weekly featured an image of the opening week at the fair. In the distance, beacons of light beckon the visitors streaming through the entry gates.

Yerkes telescope that focuses the light from Arcturus 240,000,000,000,000, miles away.

opposite
To entice visitors, fair organizers claimed that the Yerkes Observatory telescope in Wisconsin collected the light of the star Arcturus and transmitted the signal to Chicago to turn on the fair lights. Arcturus was forty light years away, so theoretically the light originated at the same time of the 1893 Columbia Exposition in Chicago.

top, left
Keck & Keck's ten-sided House of Tomorrow contained floor-to-ceiling windows, television, an automatic dishwasher, and air conditioning. Garages on either side of the house held a personal plane and a Buckminster Fuller No. 3 Dymaxion car.

bottom, left
With its abstract and geometric forms, the Westinghouse Electric building recalled the art deco style of the 1925 Exposition Internationale des Arts Décoratifs et Industriels Modernes in Paris. The exhibit showcased modern locomotives, generators, dirigibles, and household appliances.

right and opposite
Fabricated by John Roebling & Sons, with Otis elevators, the Sky Ride carried passengers from one end of the fair to the other. The stainless steel double-decker gondolas of the Sky Ride soared across lagoons and other attractions. It consisted of twelve streamlined, stainless-steel double-decker Rocket Cars, each carrying thirty-six passengers. The support towers of the Sky Ride spanned 1,850 feet along the shores of Lake Michigan, and each car emitted steam to give riders the impression they were self-powered.

top
On the Electric Building, a bas-relief titled *The Conquest of Time and Space* embraced the optimism of the fair.

above
The Studebaker exhibit presented the world's largest automobile—over thirty-nine feet high and containing an eighty-seat theater.

opposite
The Nash Motors Building displayed sixteen car models in an illuminated glass tower. Inside, the cars revolved continuously along a belt.

ENDLESS CHAIN OF CARS

MOVING IN A TOWER OF GLASS

This is the famous "Nash Tower of Value" at the World's Fair in Chicago. A building of plate glass with a high glass tower in which Nash Sixes and Eights keep moving up and down, up and down, day and night. A dazzling spectacle.

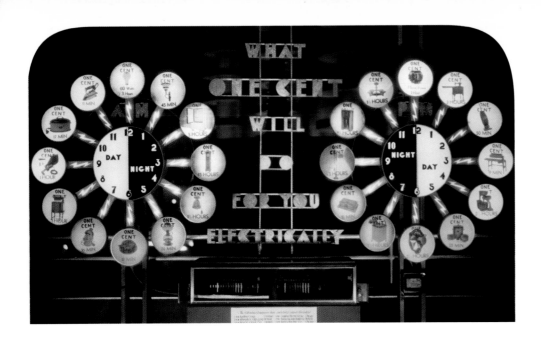

top
In the court of the Electric Building, consumers learned "what one cent will do for you electrically." Various modern household machines showed visitors the conveniences of the future.

bottom
The Hiram Walker Pavilion, designed to resemble a streamlined liquor bottle, projected four hundred feet onto a pier on the North Lagoon of Lake Michigan. Inside, it held a three-thousand-seat restaurant and a complete onsite bottling facility.

opposite
The simple curving forms of the De Soto Motors Pavilion evoked the automobiles of the day.

"CANADIAN CLUB" CAFE IN THE HIRAM WALKER EXHIBIT — "A CENTURY OF PROGRESS" — CHICAGO. 1934

LOCATED IN THE NORTH LAGOON, 16TH STREET BRIDGE

LIGHT

IS THE BEGINNING

OF ALL THINGS

FROM THE UTMOST AETHER IT ISSUES SHAPING THE STARS

ANSWERING IN ITS PATTERNS THE MAJESTY OF CREATION

left
The May 20, 1933, cover of *World's Fair Weekly* featured an abstract collage of international newspapers in the shape of a fairgoer.

below
A pamphlet for Dollar Steamship Lines touted that the fair was "not only the World's Fair but a fair share of the world itself."

opposite
Doctors and nurses demonstrated surgical techniques in a streamlined operating room with large viewing areas and sanitary surfaces. The same exhibit featured newborn babies in incubators.

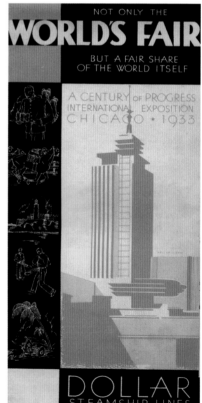

left
A Hugh Ferris rendering shows the Ford Pavilion. After the fair, it was dismantled and moved to Dearborn, Michigan.

right
The "Three-Fluted Tower" of the Federal Building represented the three branches of government: executive, legislative, and judicial.

opposite
Chicago Surface Lines brought modern modes of transportation to the city, including electric buses, trolleys, and dirigibles.

A CENTURY OF PROGRESS EXPOSITION — 1934

SEE CHICAGO

USE CHICAGO SURFACE LINES

USE CHICAGO SURFACE LINES

351- Sky Ride by Illumination, Chicago World's Fair

above
The Sky Ride became the enduring symbol of the fair.

opposite
A guidebook from 1934 features the rotating beams of light of the fair and Joseph Urban's new saturated color palette, designed for the fair's second year.

PARIS 1937

THE LAST OF PARIS'S FIVE EXPOSITIONS, the 1937 fair is best remembered as a harbinger of conflicts to come. In naming the exposition, planners made a conscious decision to create an "international," as opposed to a "universal," exposition. The world's fair lost the idealistic glamour of universal values, such as science and art, and national one-upmanship and international relations became the subtexts of the exposition, forever changing the character of world's fairs.

Perhaps the fair first brings to mind the tension between the pavilions of Nazi Germany and the Soviet Union. The exposition organizers placed the Soviet Pavilion directly across from the German Pavilion, creating a face-off between these ideological rivals. The German Pavilion, designed by Albert Speer, was a five-hundred-foot-tall monolith, crowned by a sculpture of an eagle clutching a swastika in its talons. The Soviet Union's pavilion was designed by Boris Iofan, one of the architects of the Palace of the Soviets. A sculpture of a worker and a peasant woman holding a hammer and sickle topped Iofan's monumental building. Historians speculate that Speer found Iofan's drawings and designed the German Pavilion to rival Iofan's structure. Both Speer and Iofan received gold medals for their respective designs.

The Spanish Pavilion, designed by José Luis Sert, was not as overbearing or monumental, but it was equally contentious. As civil war ravaged Spain, the Spanish Pavilion exhibited Joan Miró's *The Reaper* and Pablo Picasso's *Guernica*. These somber reminders of the tragedies of war are among the most moving images about civil war and conflict.

After the uproar over the Pavilion of the New Spirit in the 1925 Paris exposition, Le Corbusier was banned from participating in the 1937 Paris exposition. Nevertheless, with a group of acolytes, he set up an exhibition at the entrance to the exposition with plans and models for the ideal city of the future. This defiant act only augmented Le Corbusier's fame.

Other pavilions caused less controversy. The Palace of Air, designed by Audoul, Hartwig & Gérodias, resembled an airplane hangar and evoked the movement of flight. Alvar Aalto designed the Finnish Pavilion with lashed wooden poles as supports. Mock villages and live ethnographic exhibitions displayed the colonial possessions of many of the participating countries. The United States and Czechoslavakia presented elegant glass towers. The Japanese architect Junzo Sakakura, working at the time in Le Corbusier's office in Paris, established in the Japanese Pavilion one of the first genuine structures in the tradition of non-Western architecture. The tremendous design efforts of the many architects and artists would be dismantled shortly after the fair. Less than two years after the fair, Paris would be occupied by Nazi Germany, and there would never again be a world's fair in Paris.

previous page
An early conceptual design for the 1937 Paris exposition, illustrated by André Maire, featured gondolas on the Seine with the Eiffel Tower in the background.
Courtesy of The Illustration.

above
The vast main hall of the Palace of Air resembled an airplane hangar. Radial airplane engines on pedestals were displayed as modern sculptures. In the center, giant aluminum rings—suggestive of the rings of Saturn—encircled the Pontex 63 fighter plane. Robert and Sonia Delaunay designed the rings, and French architects Alfred Audoul, René Hartwig, and Jack Gérodias designed the pavilion.
Courtesy of The Illustration.

opposite, top
The vast glass facade of the Palace of Air showcased the Pontex 63 plane hanging inside.
Courtesy of The Illustration.

opposite, bottom
The Palace of Air stood in stark contrast to the classical architecture that dominated fairgrounds.

previous spread, left
Passersby paused to stare at the film-strip ornament and the grand stairway of the Photo Cine Building.

previous spread, right
The Czechoslovakian Pavilion, designed by Kreskar, seemed to float above the fairgrounds with its frosted glass facade and radio tower.

opposite
The planetarium roof evoked both the curvature of the atmosphere and Etienne-Louis Boullée's design for a Cenotaph for Newton.

left
The Palace of Discovery featured giant electrostatic machines.
Courtesy of The Illustration.

left
The Canadian Pavilion evoked the austere grain silos that populate the Canadian landscape. The Eiffel Tower stood behind the pavilion.

right
A giant stone eagle clutching a swastika in its talons topped the foreboding column of the German Pavilion, placed directly across from the equally imposing Soviet Pavilion. There was a symbolic face-off between these two ideological opponents.

NEW YORK

1939/1940

IN 1935, IN THE DEPTHS OF THE GREAT DE-
PRESSION, a group of New York business-
men and public officials led by Robert
Moses and Grover Whalen decided to
create an international exposition to
bolster the local economy. As an example, they cited Chicago's wildly successful 1933 exposition. Choosing a site in
Flushing Meadows, Queens, over a for-
mer ash pit, they began planning how
to give Americans a window into the
future. "The World of Tomorrow" was
the official theme, and sixty nations and
twenty-four states agreed to participate.

60

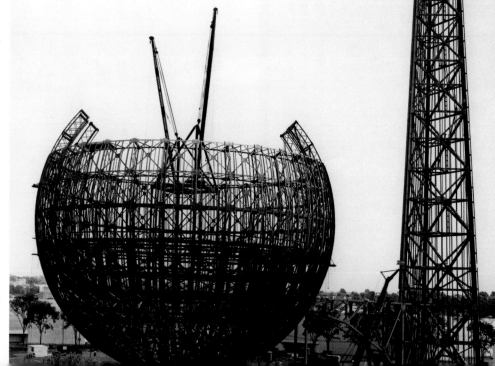

In total, corporations, states, nations, and fair organizers built more than one hundred exhibition halls in Flushing Meadows. Over the two seasons the fair was open, more than forty-five million people traveled to Queens to marvel at the wonders of the future.

For the centerpieces of the fair, organizers commissioned the seven-hundred-foot-tall Trylon and the spherical Perisphere. A nine-hundred-foot-long elevated ramp, called the Helicene, connected the Trylon to the Perisphere. Visitors ascended the ramp into the Perisphere, where they could view the "Democracity" exhibit. Designed by Henry Dreyfuss, Democracity posited a world of mega-cities connected by advanced transportation networks. In the General Motors Pavilion, the "Futurama" exhibit and ride, designed by Norman Bel Geddes, took this concept further by proposing an infinite network of superhighways and vast suburbs. Though they proved to be prophetic, at the time the Futurama and Democracity exhibits seemed as fanciful as the buildings in which they were housed. The Ford Building included a monumental spiral ramp continuously traversed by thirty-six Fords as a symbol of the Road to Tomorrow.

By encouraging innovative ideas and exhibits, the exposition showcased the era's spirit of experimentation and the prowess of American design. Eminent designers such as Raymond Loewy, Walter Dorwin Teague, Russel Wright, and Donald Deskey contributed projects ranging in scale from streamlined pencil sharpeners to double-decker super planes. The fair displayed one of the first televisions, a keyboard-operated voice synthesizer, the streamlined Chrysler Airflow, and Elektro, the Moto-Man robot that could speak and count on his own fingers. These inventions, ranging from the now everyday to the far-fetched, introduced the public to the potentials of the world of tomorrow.

For the people of tomorrow, organizers buried a time capsule to be opened in five thousand years. When the time capsule is opened, the citizens of 6939 will find the writings of Albert Einstein and Thomas Mann, a pack of Camel cigarettes, a Kewpie doll, and millions of pages of text on microfilm.

During the second year of the fair, World War II broke out, and several countries did not reopen their pavilions, including the Soviet Union. A terrorist attack on the British Pavilion killed two policemen and led to the closure of the pavilion. Though it was initially vastly popular, world events intruded and stymied the optimism and joy of the fair. It would be eighteen years before the next international exposition.

previous spread, left and right
The seven-hundred-foot-tall Trylon and spherical
Perisphere, designed by Wallace K. Harrison and
J. André Fouilhoux, became enduring icons of the
1939 New York World's Fair. The Helicene ramp
encircled the Trylon and Perisphere and led visitors
to the Democracity exhibit inside the Perisphere. Designed by Henry Dreyfuss, the Democracity exhibit
suggested a world full of mega-cities connected by
innovative transportation networks.

above
An early proposal for the Trylon and
Perisphere.

above
Skidmore and Owings designed the stainless-steel
Swift Meat Pavilion.

opposite
Commemorative stamps.

RODMAN STREET WALK

ADMINISTRATION BUILDING

FOOD NO. 3 BUILDING

PRODUCTION AND DISTRIBUTION BUILDING

MITHRANA

HOME FURNISHINGS BUILDING

TEXTILES BUILDING

PALESTINE PAVILION

DUPONT BUILDING

AVIATION

STATUE OF GEORGE WASHINGTON

ADMIRAL BYRD'S PENGUIN ISLAND

VIEW OF THE COURT OF STATES

ELECTRICAL PRODUCTS BUILDING

Y. M. C. A. BUILDING

PERISPHERE AND TRYLON

HORTICULTURAL EXHIBIT

RADIO CORPORATION OF AMERICA BUILDING

CONSUMERS BUILDING

GAS INDUSTRIES BUILDING

FORD BUILDING

left
The General Electric Power Tower display.

opposite
"Walter Dorwin Teague forecasts near nudity. What with universal air conditioning and better bodies, clothes will be reduced to a minimum."
    –*Vogue*, February 1, 1939
For this dress, Teague combined cellophane and opaque "Teca" fabric, and he constructed the shoes of Dupont Lucite.
Bruehl / *Vogue*, © Condé Nast Publications, Inc.

6

left
"Henry Dreyfuss designs for a 2000 A.D. doll... women will still want to be dolls at night... a transparent net top and stone studded tube bracelets. Her personal fan—an ingenuous combination of compact and fan."

–*Vogue*, February 1, 1939
Bruehl / *Vogue*, © Condé Nast Publications, Inc.

below
The New York Central J-3 Hudson Steamliner locomotive, designed by Henry Dreyfuss, stood outside the Railroad Pavilion.

right
This 1936 conceptual drawing of the New York World's Fair was shown to prospective exhibitors.

following spread
Raymond Loewy's Rocketport was "a dramatic visualization of the possibility of swift travel over long distances by rocketship," according to a press release. The theory behind the Rocketport was that a compressed air system gun could project objects through space. The press release elaborated that the Rocketport demonstrated "trans-ocean transport through the stratosphere by rocket."

left
A 1940 Chrysler Motors brochure showed the Rocketport, which could accommodate up to a thousand viewers at each presentation.

right
Donald Deskey, the creator of the interior of Radio City Music Hall, designed the Hall of Communications and its graphics.
Hall of Communications design, 1939 World's Fair, New York
Donald Deskey, American, 1894–1989
The Donald Deskey Collection, Cooper-Hewitt, National Design Museum, Smithsonian Institution

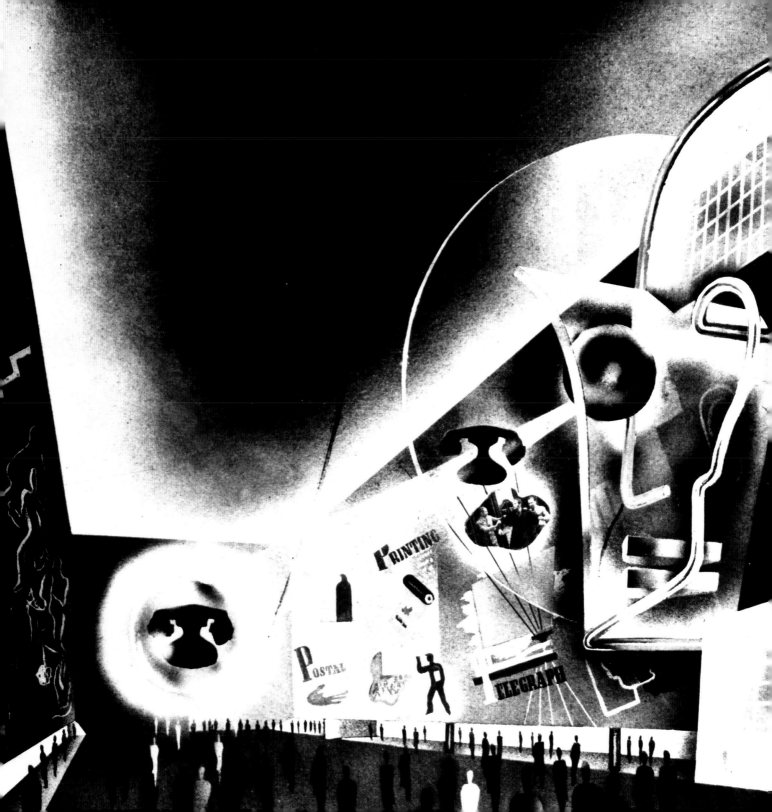

New York World's Fair 1939

A-24

above
The Westinghouse Electric Building, designed by Skidmore and Owings, showcased the latest technological developments in mechanical and electrical science. The 150-foot-tall tower in the center marked the location of a time capsule.

right
Charles F. Kettering, General Motors vice president in charge of research, appeared on the screen in the first demonstration of what might be termed the "television-telephone." By means of this equipment, which was the first of its kind ever operated in this country, Ernest L. Foss could see the person to whom he was talking. The apparatus was displayed at the formal opening of Previews of Progress, General Motors Research's stage show at the fair.

opposite
Inside of the Perisphere was Democracity, designed by Henry Dreyfuss. Visitors could peer down into the vast diorama, which contained a high-rise commercial core called "Centeron," industry in "Millvilles," and people living surrounded by greenery in "Pleasantvilles." High-speed elevated highways connected all the cities of Democracity.

left
The United States Steel Building held exhibits promoting the many innovative uses of steel. Designed by Walter Dorwin Teague and executed by architects York and Sawyer, the building was most notable for its stainless steel hemisphere and for its exposed steel structural system.

below
The Trylon and Perisphere.

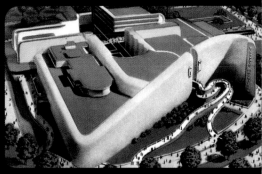

previous spread
In the General Motors' Futurama, visitors sat in continuously moving, sound-equipped chairs to view the model of 1960 America by Norman Bel Geddes.

left
Futurama at the General Motors Pavilion was the most popular exhibit at the fair. Lines continuously snaked up the ramp, and visitors received buttons that read "I have seen the future."

above
The General Motors Pavilion was designed by Albert Kahn with interiors by Norman Bel Geddes.

right
Donald Deskey's Trans-Lux proposal incorporated stainless steel and neon lights.
Trans Lux Theatre Entry design, 1939 World's Fair, New York
Donald Deskey, American, 1894–1989
The Donald Deskey Collection, Cooper-Hewitt, National Design Museum, Smithsonian Institution

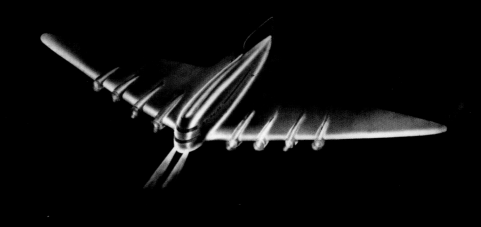

left
Echoing the Wonder Bread bags, the Continental Baking Company Building featured colorful round buttons.

above
"Faster, safer, and more powerful!" The eight-engine double-decker airplane of the future, as imagined by Raymond Loewy, was the focal point of the Transportation Building.

right
A proposal for the Aviation Pavilion by William Lescaze.

left
A 1936 proposal imagined multi-tiered ramps filled with fairgoers.

right
"Gilbert Rhode banishes buttons, pockets, collars, ties. The man of the next century will revolt against shaving and wear a beautiful beard, says the designer of boilers, pianos, clocks, and metal furniture. His hat will be an antennae−snatching radio out of the ether. His socks disposable, his suit minus tie collar and buttons."
– *Vogue*, February 1, 1939
Bruehl / *Vogue*, © Condé Nast Publications, Inc.

left
The woman of tomorrow, dressed in a clear plastic skirt, stretches her arms toward the promise of the future.

right
This robot wowed visitors by counting to five.

left
"Better things for Better Living . . . through Chemistry."
The Du Pont Pavilion, a 105-foot multicolored tower,
was meant to evoke a child's chemistry kit. At night
the changing colored lights simulated the bubbling of
chemicals. Inside was a demonstration of spinning nylon—a new invention that premiered at the fair. Walter
Dorwin Teague designed the tower with R. J. Harper
and A. M. Erickson.

right
The Inventions Building, with its gently curved metal facade, displayed the era's spirit of experimentation and
the advances of American design.

above
Wearing a transparent beach coat made of "synthetic glass," "Miss Futurama" Betty Crain presents a model of a streamlined automobile to Harvey Gibson, chairman of the board of the New York World's Fair.

right
For Ford-Mercury-Lincoln, an abstract steel sculpture by Robert Foster featured the winged messenger Mercury holding a "V" and an "8," promoting the new powerful engines.

ROME

PLANNED WITH DIRECT INVOLVEMENT BY BENITO MUSSOLINI, the 1942 exposition was part of an ambitious plan to develop a new satellite city southwest of Rome. Timed to commemorate the twentieth anniversary of fascist rule in Italy, the fair was to showcase the grandeur of Rome's past and future. It was called the Esposizione Universale di Roma (EUR). When World War II broke out, the exposition was delayed and later was cancelled when Mussolini's government collapsed.

The bold plan, developed by chief architect Marcello Piacentini in collaboration with Mussolini, called for an ideal city filled with modern counterparts to ancient Roman structures. Buildings would be made in modern materials with more "pure" geometries, and their scale and purpose would mirror the fabled buildings of ancient Rome. Much of the infrastructure and a few significant buildings were completed before the war erupted, including the Palace of Italian Civilization and the Museum of Roman Civilization. Perforated with arches, the Palace of Italian Civilization is essentially a square version of the Colosseum. Similarly, the Museum of Roman Civilization is a

modern interpretation of an imperial Roman building with forty-foot-high travertine columns and skylit galleries. An obelisk commemorating Guglielmo Marconi, the inventor of the wireless telegraph, was proposed but never built. Adalberto Libera planned a giant parabolic arch as the symbol of the fair, and though never completed, it appeared on publicity posters and postcards. The proposed arch bore a striking resemblance to the Gateway Arch designed by Eero Saarinen. Libera, according to the historian Thomas Schumacher, became enraged when he saw the Gateway Arch design and threatened to sue Saarinen. Cesare Pascoletti also proposed an arch as a monument to fascism. The imposing forms of the EUR possibly explain why the satellite city never fully developed and even now remains a desolate suburb of Rome.

While the fair was being planned, the editor of the Italian design magazine *Casabella* accused Piacentini of being a "jumped-up Vitruvius" who was forfeiting good taste for "the most grotesque exhibitionism." Although it never achieved what Mussolini and Piacentini envisioned and was perhaps "grotesque," the EUR was one of the most ambitious planning efforts undertaken for an exposition.

brussels '58

AFTER THE DEVASTATIONS of World War II, Expo '58 in Brussels signaled the return of international fairs, groundbreaking art and design, and greater international stability. With the theme "Building the World on a Human Scale," the exposition promoted peace among nations, faith in technological progress, innovation in art and design, and a general optimism about the modern world. In its brief six-month run, the Brussels fair attracted forty-two million visitors and produced pioneering works of art and design.

Towering over the fairgrounds, the Atomium was the symbol of the fair—a 335-foot-high model of an iron molecule. This was 165 billion times the size of an actual iron crystal. Nine aluminum spheres, sixty feet in diameter, were supported in the structure. Windows in the top sphere offered visitors panoramic views of the fair and Brussels, and the other eight spheres contained exhibits. Escalators in gargantuan tubes connected the spheres and transported visitors through the exhibits. Designed by Belgian engineer Andre Waterkeyn with Andre and Jean Polak, the Atomium was to last only for the duration of the fair, but it proved so popular that city officials decided to keep the Atomium as a city symbol. It has become a national icon, and a renovation was completed in 2006.

The pavilions similarly experimented with innovative structures and materials. Resembling a large flying saucer, the U.S. Pavilion was, at the time, the world's largest circular building. The Civil Engineering Pavilion featured a cantilevered concrete arm. The French Pavilion, designed by Guillaume Gillet, Rene Sargent, and Jean Prouvé, was an innovative double-winged space frame. Le Corbusier and Iannis Xenakis designed the Philips Pavilion, a masterwork of steel cables and concrete. Composed of twelve hyperbolic parabolas, the Philips Pavilion was constructed entirely of cables and a skin of small concrete slabs. For the space inside, Edgar Varèse composed the "Poème Electronique," which played on 425 speakers. At the time, the music was spectacularly unpopular, but it greatly influenced many later composers and musicians. Le Corbusier tested the plasticity of concrete structures, inspiring later generations with his forms as well as the structural innovations of the pavilion. The "Poème Electronique" is considered a forerunner to contemporary electronic music. Vastly unpopular, the speakers and pavilion were destroyed the day after the fair closed, and unfortunately the "Poème Electronique" can no longer be heard in the spectacular space for which it was composed.

Part of the appeal—and the anxiety—of world's fairs is their ephemeral nature. Like the Philips Pavilion and "Poème Electronique," they often disappear, leaving almost no trace except photographs and memories. On the other hand, the short international exposition gave architects, designers, composers, and artists an extraordinary amount of freedom to experiment, and it introduced the public to revolutionary art and design. All that physically remains of Expo '58 is the Atomium, but the innovations of Le Corbusier, Edgar Varèse, and the many other artists and designers continue to influence contemporary artists, composers, and designers.

opposite
The Atomium is now a beloved Brussels icon.

previous spread, left
Composed of twelve hyperbolic parabolas, the Philips Pavilion had no supporting columns. Designed by Le Corbusier and Iannis Xenakis, it used cables in tension against a skin of small concrete slabs.

previous spread, right
For inside the Philips Pavilion, Edgar Varèse composed "Poème Electronique," which played on 425 speakers. Viewers watched films of nuclear explosions while listening to Varèse's composition. One of the forerunners of contemporary electronic music, "Poème Electronique" was a combination of random electronic sounds and "musique concrète."

left
Fireworks exploded around the 335-foot-tall Atomium, the iconic centerpiece of the 1958 Brussels exposition. A model of an iron molecule at 165 billion times the actual size, the Atomium remains a beloved Brussels landmark.

right
From inside the Atomium, visitors could view the fairgrounds.

above
Egon Eiermann designed the German Pavilion.

bottom, left
A five-pointed star was the symbol of the fair. Each point of the star represented a continent.

bottom, right
Stamps from 1958 depicted artificial satellites circling the Earth.

opposite
Le Corbusier's Philips Pavilion was demolished the day after the exposition ended.

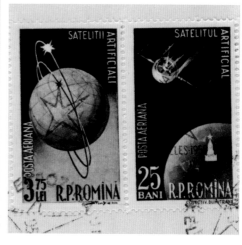

opposite
At the time the largest circular building in the world, the U.S. Pavilion was meant to present American society as open and welcoming. The pavilion, designed by Edward Durell Stone, was a gigantic polygonal structure with thirty-six sides.

above
Based on a concept by the sculptor Jacques Moeschal, the architect J. Van Doosselaere and the engineer A. Paduart designed the soaring concrete forms of the Civil Engineering Pavilion.

above
Architects H. Lobb & Partners, J. Ratcliff, and J. Gardner designed the faceted facade of the British Pavilion.

right
Belgian postal stamps featured the Atomium and Benelux Pavilion.

opposite
At the center of the U.S. Pavilion, two circular frames, each twenty meters in diameter, were separated by 8.5 meters and connected to the structure by more than one hundred cables. An opening in the roof allowed an internal pool to collect rainwater.

MOSCOW '59

ORGANIZED, ASSEMBLED, AND SENT TO MOSCOW by the United States Information Agency, the American National Exhibition in Moscow was intended to showcase the American way of life and the freedom Americans had in expressing themselves. Ironically, the one American art exhibit among the many science, technology, and culture exhibits was nearly derailed by Congressman Francis Walter, chair of the House Committee on Un-American Activities. He accused more than half the artists of being communist sympathizers. Walter went as far as convening congressional hearings to remove the art exhibition from Moscow. He failed, but his attempts belied the American effort to portray themselves as proponents of freedom.

The centerpiece of the exhibition was a geodesic dome designed by Buckminster Fuller. Inside the dome, a film produced by Charles and Ray Eames played. The film, called *Glimpses of the U.S.A.*, illustrated a day in the life of the United States with more than 2,200 changing images of people, buildings, technology, and automobiles on seven twenty-by-thirty-

foot screens. It was one of the first multiscreen films ever made, and Charles Eames later said, "Multiple projection of images . . . was not simply a trick; it was a method to employ all the viewer's senses. The reinforcement by multiple images made the American Story seem credible."

Held at the zenith of the cold war, the Moscow exhibition was the site of the infamous "kitchen debate" between Vice President Richard Nixon and Soviet Premier Nikita Khrushchev. It took place in the kitchen of a model American home, displaying the latest in American household gadgetry. The public discussion was ostensibly about sharing knowledge of the daily lives of Americans, but with tension high between the two superpowers, it became increasingly heated.

Though not a world's fair in any traditional sense, the American National Exhibition was emblematic of cold war–era expositions. Bravado and national competition became more important than scientific or artistic progress. The art exhibition was nearly censored, the Eames multiscreen film was funded by the United States Information Agency, and, even in the seemingly innocuous setting of a model kitchen, world leaders tensely discussed the relative merits of capitalism and communism.

left
In a geodesic dome by Buckminster Fuller, a film produced by Charles and Ray Eames played across seven twenty-by-thirty-foot screens.

above
An exhibition pamphlet featured the Sputnik capsule.

'62

THE SEATTLE WORLD'S FAIR—also known as Century 21—gave visitors and Seattle's citizens a glimpse of the future. Fair planners had been searching for a theme when the Soviets successfully launched Sputnik in 1957. It was the beginning of the space race between the United States and the Soviet Union, and suddenly science and the space age became a national obsession. Titled "Man's Life in the Space Age," this was the first world's fair in the United States since World War II, and it drew

SEATTLE

almost ten million people in its short six-month run.

The space race preoccupied all Americans—from political leaders to schoolchildren—and the Century 21 fair was considered the ideal showcase for American advances in science and technology. When the Soviet Union displayed the Sputnik satellite, NASA countered with the Friendship 7 capsule in its pavilion. American companies such as the Ford Motor Company and Boeing developed space-themed exhibits. Ford exhibited "An Adventure in Outer Space," and Boeing presented the "Spacearium," which took visitors on an imaginary ten-minute trip to outer space. The "World of Tomorrow" exhibit, designed by Donald Deskey, had perhaps the most fantastical entrance: fairgoers reached the exhibit through a giant one-hundred-passenger clear spherical elevator called the Bubbleator. In the United States Space Pavilion, designed by Minoru Yamasaki, Charles and Ray Eames's film *The House of Science* premiered. The public's interest in science and space had never been stronger, and exhibitors strove to show fairgoers what science promised for the future.

Not simply future-oriented, the Century 21 exposition had an immediate effect on Seattle's infrastructure and skyline. It produced such lasting Seattle icons as the Space Needle and the Monorail. The fair site was more than a mile away from downtown Seattle, and the fair planners commissioned the Swedish manufacturer Alweg Rapid Transit Systems to construct the 1.3-mile-long Monorail to transport visitors across the city. Some planners envisioned that after the fair, the Monorail could be extended throughout the region. The Space Needle towered over the fair site at 605 feet tall. At the time, it was the tallest structure west of Chicago, and it quickly became a symbol for Seattle.

Reflecting on the impact of the fair on Seattle, Joe Gandy, president of the fair, said, "[The Fair] has rekindled civic spirit . . . the spirit that built a community out of ashes, that moved hills and spanned lakes and waterways and sent its commerce around the world." The Century 21 fair announced Seattle's emergence as a major American city, put forth America's vision for the space age, and introduced Seattle to its future.

previous spread
While visiting Stuttgart, Seattle World's Fair Commission chair Edward E. Carlson dined in a restaurant in the city's broadcast tower. Taken with the city views and the symbolism of the tower, Carlson decided that Seattle's fair needed a similar "restaurant in the sky." The architect John Graham Jr. was hired to design Seattle's Space Needle partly because Graham's previous experience included a revolving restaurant in Honolulu.

right
At Minoru Yamasaki's U.S. Science Pavilion, aluminum pointed arches topped a U-shaped configuration of six connected buildings. Yamasaki is perhaps best known as the architect of the World Trade Center in New York.

opposite, left
A drawing of the Space Needle.

opposite, right
A cutaway view reveals the inner workings of the Space Needle.

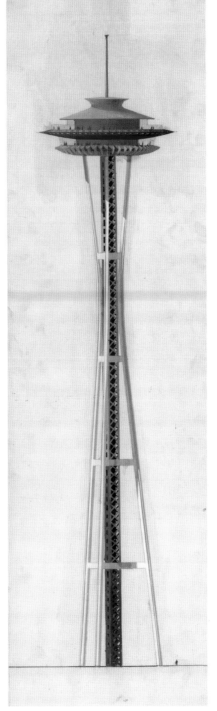

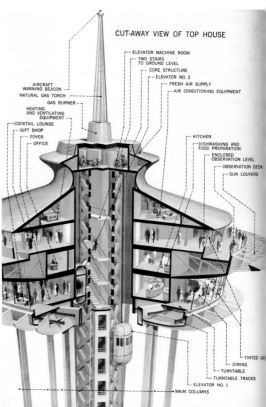

CUT-AWAY VIEW OF TOP HOUSE

ELEVATOR MACHINE ROOM
TWO STAIRS TO GROUND LEVEL
CORE STRUCTURE
ELEVATOR NO. 2
FRESH AIR SUPPLY
AIR CONDITIONING EQUIPMENT

AIRCRAFT WARNING BEACON
NATURAL GAS TORCH
GAS BURNER
HEATING AND VENTILATING EQUIPMENT
COCKTAIL LOUNGE
GIFT SHOP
FOYER
OFFICE

KITCHEN
DISHWASHING AND FOOD PREPARATION
ENCLOSED OBSERVATION LEVEL
OBSERVATION DECK
SUN LOUVERS

TINTED G
DINING
TURNTABLE
TURNTABLE TRACKS
ELEVATOR NO. 1
MAIN COLUMNS

bells on **hiGh-Fi**

Memorable Music played on
World's largest Carillon
The 538 Bell Schulmerich
"Carillon Americana"® Bells
Instrument by John Klein

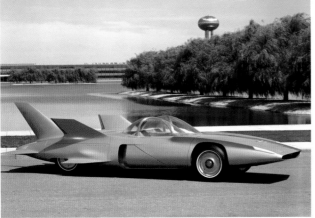

previous spread, left
Early study models of Donald Deskey's exhibit hall featured cubes suspended like a "floating city."
Architectural model of 1962 "World of Tomorrow" exhibit, 1962 World's Fair, Seattle
Donald Deskey Associates
The Donald Deskey Collection, Cooper-Hewitt, National Design Museum, Smithsonian Institution

previous spread, right
The Bubbleator, a gigantic bubble-shaped hydraulic elevator, carried one hundred people at a time to the World of Tomorrow exhibit. "First floor," the operator announced, "threats, thresholds, frustrations and fulfillments, challenges and opportunities."

opposite
A 45 rpm record jacket features an image of the Space Needle with downtown Seattle in the background.

above
Donald Deskey Associates proposed a "Century 21" city complete with an indoor monorail.
Rendering for a "Century 21" city with indoor monorail, 1962 World's Fair, Seattle
Donald Deskey Associates
The Donald Deskey Collection, Cooper-Hewitt, National Design Museum, Smithsonian Institution

left
The GM Firebird III prototype more closely resembled a land-based rocket than an automobile. Plastic fighter jet domes over the passenger area limited wind resistance, and large aircraft fins in the rear deflected air currents.

left
A United States Postal Service four-cent stamp featured the monorail traveling past the Space Needle.
Reprinted with permission of the United States Postal Service. All Rights Reserved.

right
A fair hostess explained the large-scale model of a DNA molecule at the U.S. Science Pavilion.

opposite
A rendering by Donald Deskey Associates imagines the Bubbleator approaching the "World of Tomorrow" exhibit.
Rendering of "Bubbleator" inside "World of Tomorrow" exhibit, 1962 World's Fair, Seattle
Donald Deskey Associates
The Donald Deskey Collection, Cooper-Hewitt, Smithsonian Institution

SPACE NEEDLE

UNITED STATES SCIENCE PAVILION

left
The main attraction at Ford's "Adventure in Outer Space" was a simulated journey into space aboard a one-hundred-foot spacecraft. Visitors could view animated models of satellites, the Earth, moon, and planets from their "flight seats."

above
The Space Needle and U.S. Science Pavilion adorned souvenirs ranging from matchbooks to posters.

below
In the U.S. Science Pavilion, a three-dimensional display depicted orbiting satellites and distant universes.

right
Visitors peered into rocket boosters in the U.S. Science Pavilion. Much of the actual mechanicals were hidden from visitors to prevent loss of important technological secrets to rival countries.

LAUSANNE '64

"The most beautiful fair in this century—the National Exposition at Lausanne . . . was an exemplary work of art, excitingly varied and yet harmonious." —Wolf von Eckardt, *Time*, May 3, 1982

ALTHOUGH NOT AN INTERNATIONAL EXPOSITION in accordance with the Bureau of International Expositions, the Swiss National Fair of 1964 was a showplace for innovative architecture, art, and technology, and, perhaps foremost, an effort to represent Switzerland and Swiss identity in a global context. The Swiss Military Building, resembling a concrete hedgehog with 141 sharp points, emphasized military strength and independence. In front of the Military Building stood a three-pointed, missile-shaped sculpture. In the Food, Beverage, and Tobacco Pavilion, flying shopping baskets carried visitors through the food displays. Huge sausages, chocolates, cookies, and other traditional Swiss foods hung from the ceiling. Fairgoers could explore the depths of Lake Geneva in Auguste Piccard's submersible vessel, the Mésoscaphe. In the South Pacific, the Mésoscaphe set the then record for the deepest recorded underwater ocean dive in history—more than thirty thousand feet below sea level. In Lake Geneva, the trip was far shallower. An open-air monorail took fairgoers under, over, and through fair buildings. The master architect of the exposition, Alberto Camenzind, said, "Expo '64 took place at a time of peace and prosperity. Our task was to present a picture of the Swiss." We were asked, "Was Switzerland a nation? Are we a large group of people that thinks alike?" The exposition showed the Swiss and the world that it was a nation with a cohesive, independent identity.

opposite
The Swiss Military Building resembled a concrete hedgehog with 141 sharp points.

opposite
An op art exhibition.

above
In space suits—perhaps even dressed as aliens from outer space—fair participants paraded to the delight of fairgoers.

new york '64

PERHAPS MOST NOTABLE for reflecting American corporate power, the 1964 New York World's Fair was dedicated to "Man's Achievement on a Shrinking Globe in an Expanding Universe." Located at Flushing Meadows, it was the largest fair ever held in the United States. With exhibits from General Motors, IBM, Du Pont, and Kodak among others, corporations dominated the fair, and corporate support was even responsible for its centerpiece — U.S. Steel built the twelve-story Unisphere. The theme reflected the concerns of the cold war and the hope of new technologies to conquer the universe, bring peace, and ease everyday life.

Robert Moses, then the New York City Parks Commissioner, was the corporate president of the fair. Following his involvement with New York's previous world's fair, Moses became determined to finish Flushing Meadows Park and believed that a second world's fair could provide the funding and incentive to finally complete the park. Gordon Bunshaft of Skidmore, Owings & Merrill was the original head of the fair's design, and he proposed clustering all the pavilions inside a giant donut-shaped dome. Eventually, he resigned in frustration because Moses was focused on maximizing profits using more economical building methods and reusing the master plan, infrastructure, and roads from the 1939 fair.

It was not an officially sanctioned fair, and many countries, including several European nations, Canada, and the Soviet Union, chose not to participate. Moses believed it was not necessary to work within the Bureau of International Exhibions guidelines, which required free rent to participating nations. To make up r the deficit of national pavilions, Moses recruited corporations, individual U.S. ates, and many Asian, South and Central American countries. Drawing upon his ng career building highways and roads, Moses even convinced automobile and etroleum companies to participate, including Uniroyal Tire, Sinclair, Esso Gaso- ne, and the Detroit automakers.

For the fair's centerpiece, U.S. Steel built and paid for the Unisphere, a giant odel of the earth. Earlier, Paul Rudolph proposed a tilted, saucerlike structure illed the "Galaxion" as the symbol. Walter Dorwin Teague suggested the "Jour- ey to the Stars," a 170-foot aluminum and steel spiral with helium balloons ating above.

Ultimately, despite the Unisphere, corporate support, and Moses's cost-cut- ng measures, the fair lost money and attracted only fifty-one million people—far ort of the projected seventy million. In an effort to boost profits the second year, oses allowed fifty-eight bars to open on the fairgrounds but even alcohol could ot lure more fairgoers.

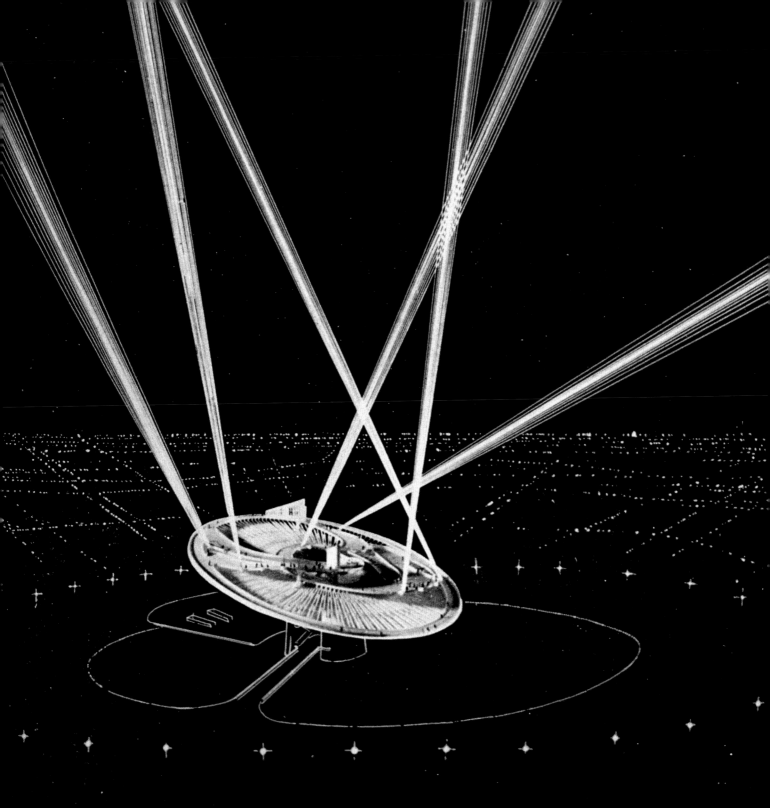

opposite
From the Swiss Pavilion, the Skyride carried fairgoers 1,875 feet in open-air gondolas.

left
The world's most powerful searchlight rose from the center of the Electric Power and Light Pavilion. The building consisted of six hundred aluminum prisms that reflected the varying colored lights.

below
The Unisphere was the symbol of the fair and remains standing in Flushing Meadows.

following spread, left
In the Bell Pavilion, bubble-shaped telephone booths obscured the heads of users.

following spread, right
The Tent of Tomorrow at the New York Pavilion was the largest suspended roof in the world. Light flooded the floor through transparent panels in the roof. The main floor featured a terrazzo map of the state of New York.
Photo: Ezra Stoller © Esto

left
The Brass Rail Restaurant, designed by architect Victor A. Lundy, stood in front of the New York Pavilion. The roof of the Brass Rail Restaurant was held aloft by giant balloons.

below
The School of Tomorrow, proposed by Frederic P. Wiedersum Associates, suspended cylindrical classrooms from a central core with cables. The firm has been established since 1926 and is now known as Wiedersum Associates Architects.

following spread
Designed by Philip Johnson with Norman Foster, the three observation towers of the New York Pavilion soared above the fair at 226 feet. Inside, the "Sky Streak" elevators carried visitors to the observation platforms.

opposite
Hoping to re-create the magic of the Futurama exhibit at the 1939 New York World's Fair, General Motors developed an updated Futurama for the 1964 fair. This Futurama ride began at a scale model of the moon, and manned "Lunar Crawlers" traveled across the rugged moonscape.

above
The City of Tomorrow model depicted a centralized city core with satellite communities fanning outward.

left

Crowds surrounded the General Electric exhibit, which included a mock-up of controlled thermo-nuclear fusion. A GE brochure, now displayed at the Queens Museum, describes the exhibit: "A magnetic field squeezed plasma of radioactive deuterium gas for a millionth of a second at a temperature of 20 million degrees Fahrenheit. A vivid flash was the result of atoms colliding and creating a radioactive release of free energy." Geiger counters at the exhibit "confirmed" the release of radiation.

above

An orb-shaped telephone booth from Bell Systems held a Picturephone, which transmitted images as well as voices.
Courtesy of AT&T Archives and History Center

below
The General Motors Pavilion housed Futurama, an updated version of GM's wildly popular 1939 Futurama exhibit. Its 110-foot facade, designed by the General Motors styling staff, tilted forward like an immense curved windshield.

opposite, top and below
The AMF Monorail consisted of ninety-foot-long, two-car trains, which continuously circled the fair day and night.

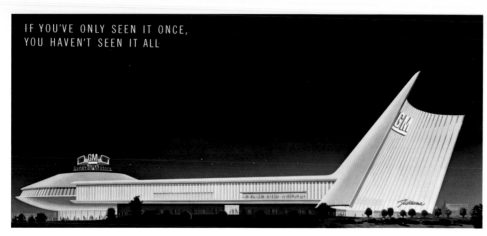

IF YOU'VE ONLY SEEN IT ONCE,
YOU HAVEN'T SEEN IT ALL

left
The profile of the GM Pavilion evoked a low automobile.

below
With its sleek lines and bright red color, the GM Futura IV resembled the General Motors Pavilion.

right, top
This GM concept car was designed to hold a modular shopping basket. The shopping cart wheels would fold up and fit neatly into the rear of the car.

right, bottom
Space travel and rocket imagery influenced the design of the Firebird IV concept car.

above
The updated Futurama exhibit suggested that humans would live and work at the bottom of the sea. A model included vacation pods, hotels, and restaurants equipped with oxygen.

right
On the Eastman Kodak Pavilion roof, a woman posed for a photograph amid the moon craters and peaks.

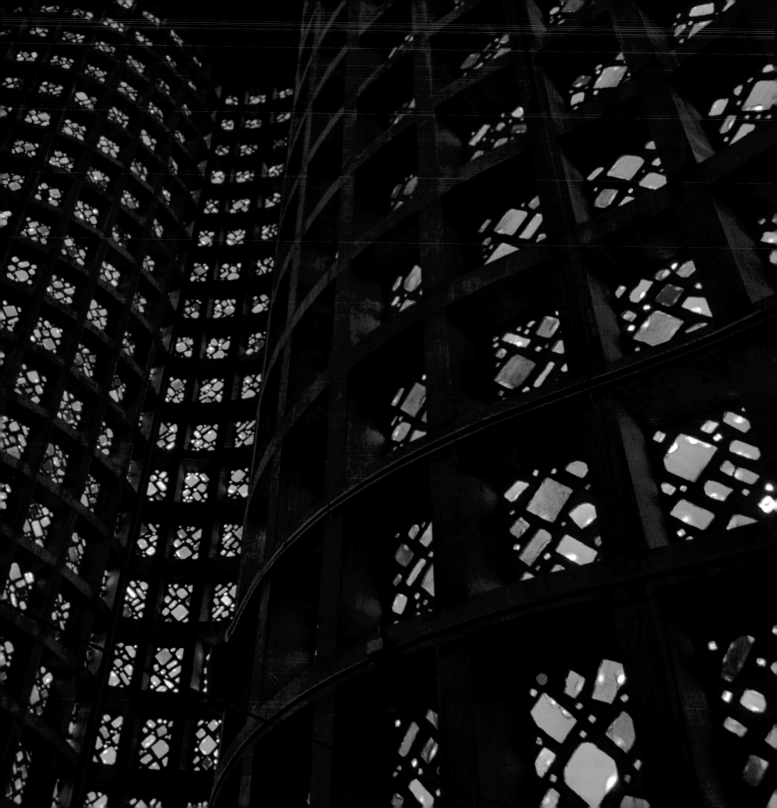

NEW YORK WORLD'S FAIR-1965
RIDE *The*
INDOOR HELICOPTERS
SEE
THE WORLD'S LARGEST MODEL OF NEW YORK CITY

left
The undulating concrete walls of the Hall of Science, designed by Wallace K. Harrison of Harrison and Abramovitz, were embedded with chunks of cobalt blue glass, creating a soft, almost reverential glow for the science exhibits contained within.

above
A miniature helicopter circled the model of New York City, and fairgoers could ride it and gaze at the model of the city.

right
Demonstrating Bell Aviation's Rocket Pack, an "astronaut" floated over delighted fairgoers.

Montreal '67

EXPO '67 IN MONTREAL introduced cutting-edge technological and structural innovations in architecture to the public, developed necessary roads and public transportation networks for Montreal, and announced Montreal's emergence as a major city. Planned to celebrate Canada's centennial, it was a critical and financial success, attracting more than fifty million visitors to Montreal in six short months—fifteen million more than had been predicted. For a fair theme, the organizers looked to the 1939 book *Terre des Hommes* by Antoine de Saint-Exupéry, author of *The Little Prince*, and titled the exposition "Man and His World."

An extensive underground metro system was developed connecting downtown Montreal to the various exposition facilities. Using the earth dug up for the metro, Mayor Jean Drapeau created man-made islands for the fairgrounds in the St. Lawrence River. Numerous roads and bridges were built to transport fair participants, dignitaries, and visitors. These islands now make up a park network in the center of the city, and the exposition left a lasting legacy of public transportation, roads, and public space.

For the United States Pavilion, Buckminster Fuller, in collaboration with the Japanese engineer Shoji Sadao, designed a geodesic dome called the Biosphere. The dome, 250 feet in diameter, drew more than five million visitors, making it one of the most popular attractions of the fair. The structure was a further development of Fuller's dome for the 1959 American National Exhibition in Moscow.

Another groundbreaking structure, developed by the Israeli-born architect Moshe Safdie, appeared on one of the man-made islands between the exposition site and downtown Montreal. Originally planned as a one-thousand-unit community complete with stores and schools, Habitat '67 never achieved that size and population. For the fair, 158 apartment units were complete and stacked together in a seemingly haphazard arrangement, perhaps inspired by the Japanese Metabolist architects. Habitat '67 was an experiment in prefabricated construction. The concrete panels were made at a factory nearby and the units were assembled on site. The simple construction could easily be expanded with new units and buildings. At the time, it was vastly unpopular, but recently Habitat has become fashionable.

Similarly, the German Pavilion experimented with structure and construction techniques. Frei Otto designed the German Pavilion as a tent structure suspended from eight tubular steel masts, covering an exhibition space of terraces. All the parts were made in Germany, shipped to Montreal, and assembled on site.

Wildly popular with the public, the expo also drew celebrities, dignitaries, and political leaders. Jackie Kennedy and Princess Grace of Monaco wandered the fairgrounds. Lyndon Johnson visited, but antiwar protesters besieged him. Charles de Gaulle was greeted more warmly, but he created controversy when he declared "Vive le Québec libre!" ("Long live a free Quebec"), which became the motto for the Quebec independence movement. Expo '67 was one of the most popular world's fairs.

above
The Venezuela Pavilion was composed of
three brightly painted cubes.

left
An expo hostess talked on a telephone covered by a plastic bubble.

above
The United States Pavilion, designed by Buckminster Fuller, was commonly known as the Biosphere.

following spread, left
Buckminster Fuller's geodesic dome, 250 feet in diameter, appeared to be a giant floating bubble. Its clear plastic skin reflected sunlight during the day and glowed from within at night. The plastic skin was destroyed in a fire during a 1976 renovation.
Photo: Night View of United States of America Pavilion, Expo 67, Montreal
© Library and Archives Canada. Reproduced with the permission of the Minister of Public Works and Government Services Canada (2006)

following spread, right
A recent photograph reveals the dome's remaining metal structure.

above and left

An experiment in prefabricated construction, Moshe Safdie's Habitat '67 complex contains 158 seemingly randomly arranged apartment blocks. A self-contained concrete factory was built near the site to allow the panels to be made close by. Situated on a man-made island between the main Expo '67 site and downtown Montreal, Habitat '67 was originally planned as a one-thousand-unit community with stores and schools. After the fair closed, it was downsized because of general lack of popularity and isolation from the city. Today, the complex (retrofitted with plastic enclosed tube hallways to brace residents against the harsh winters) has become a fashionable and sought-after address.

opposite

A row of shimmering aluminum fins encircled the concrete and steel structure of the French Pavilion. Themed "The Tradition of Invention," the French Pavilion included exhibits of atomic reactors and deep-sea prospecting.

left
From the interior balconies of the French Pavilion, visitors could view films about the cycle of life.

above
Various building technologies and materials were on display at the glass-enclosed Quebec Pavilion, the cedar-shingled Western Provinces Pavilion, and the plastic Ontario Pavilion.

The German Pavilion, designed by Frei Otto, was comprised of a cable net over eight steel masts, under which was a stretched polyester skin.

above
An expo hostess greeted visitors.
Photo: Pavilion hostess at Expo 67
© Library and Archives Canada. Reproduced with the permission of the Minister of Public Works and Government Services Canada (2006)

right
A fair hostess wore a dress in the same color scheme as the Kaleidoscope.
Photo: Hostess of the Kaleidoscope at Expo 67
© Library and Archives Canada. Reproduced with the permission of the Minister of Public Works and Government Services Canada (2006)

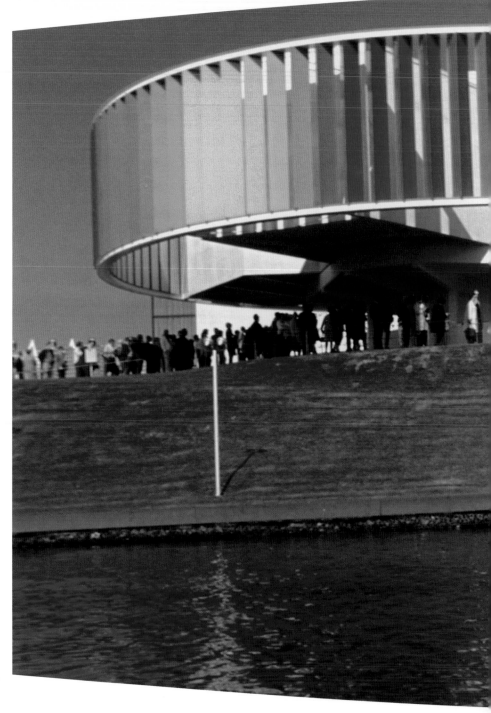

opposite
In the "Man the Explorer" exhibit, Leonardo da Vinci's famous image of a man appeared in neon lights.

above
The "Man the Explorer" Pavilions consisted of four exhibit halls in three interconnected buildings. One exhibit magnified a human cell one million times and another featured a gigantic model of a human brain that was used to explain the evolution of reflex actions.
Postcard: Thematic Pavilions, Expo 67, ca. 1963
© Canadian Corporation for the 1967 World Exhibition.
Reproduced with the permission of the Minister of Public Works and Government Services Canada (2006)

above
Fair hostesses modeled the latest fashions, including
snazzy white raincoats and multicolor hats.
Photo: Uniforms of the hostesses of Expo 67
© Library and Archives Canada. Reproduced with the per-
mission of the Minister of Public Works and Government
Services Canada (2006)

above, right
The Soviet Union Pavilion, designed by Mikhail Posokhin, and Buckminster Fuller's U.S. Pavilion stood side
by side.

opposite
In the Soviet Union Pavilion, a model of a colorful nuclear
reactor suggested the possible peaceful uses of atomic
power.

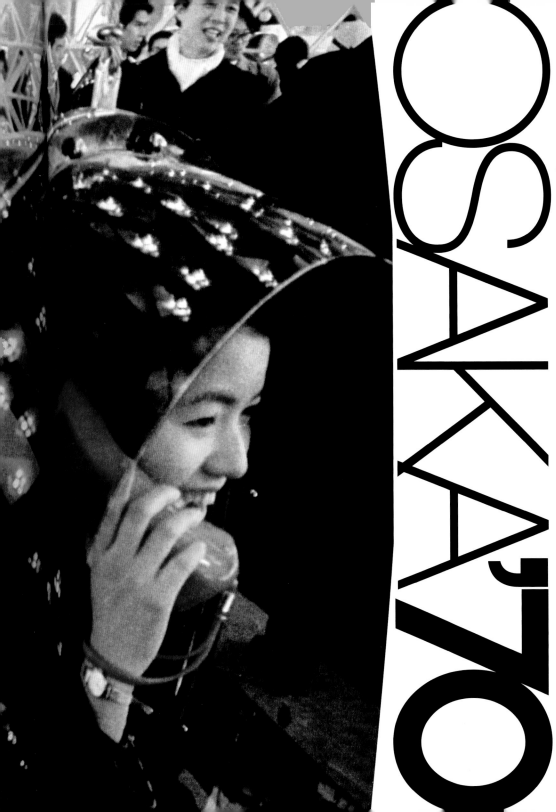

OSAKA '70

THE FIRST WORLD'S FAIR held in Asia, Expo '70 symbolized how rapidly Japan had developed since the war. Originally planned for 1940 to commemorate Japan's 2,600th year as an empire, it was postponed thirty years because of World War II. Organizers chose the Japanese architect Kenzo Tange to be the master planner of the exposition, and they found a rural bamboo forest on the outskirts of Osaka for the site. Themed "Progress and Harmony for Mankind," the exposition had seventy-seven countries participating and attracted more than sixty-four million visitors.

During the fair, a time capsule was buried on the site. To be opened in five thousand years, the time capsule would be a window into life in the twentieth century. It contained a turntable for records, a silk condom, false teeth, a micro-mini television, and tributes to the victims of the Hiroshima atomic bomb.

Like the 1964 fairs, many of the pavilions experimented with new materials, including plastics and fiberglass. The United States Pavilion employed an innovative new structure: a long-span, cable-stiffened pneumatic dome. Initially developed by NASA in 1967, the fiberglass

175

membrane used for the roof was inflated by air pressure that caused it to float above the exhibit floor. This is now a commonly used structural system for sports arenas. The pavilion, which was mostly underground, was condemned at the time—referred to as "soggy waffle and a burial mound." In spite of this, there were many popular attractions inside, including an actual moon rock brought back from Apollo 11 and Babe Ruth's baseball uniform.

Now the site is the Expo Memorial Park, and almost all the pavilions have been demolished. The centerpiece of the fairgrounds—the Tower of the Sun, designed by Okamoto Taro—still stands on the site, a lasting memento of when the world came to Osaka.

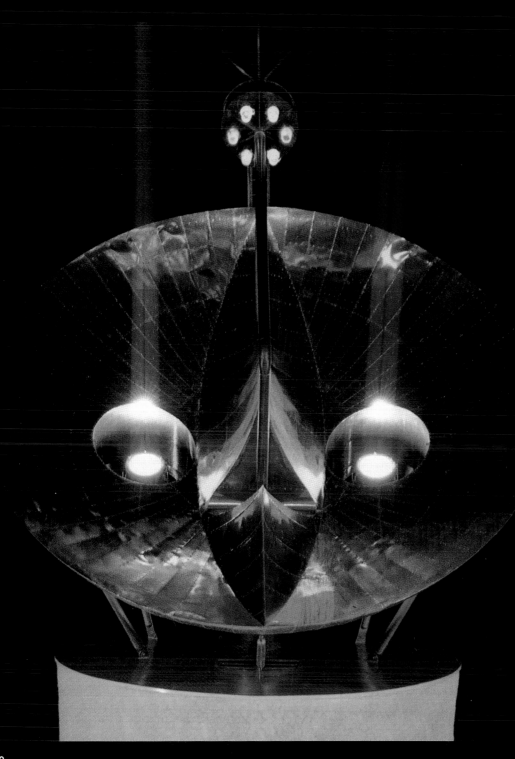

previous spread, left
Fair hostesses posed under the
Swiss Pavilion.

previous spread, right
The spiral form of the Soviet Pavilion rose to 350 feet, dwarfing
many of the neighboring pavilions.
Designed by Mikhail Posokhin, V.
Svirsky, and the engineer A. Kon-
dratyev of Mosproject, the shape
was inspired by the hammer and
sickle.

left
Illuminated at night, the Tower of
the Sun was the fair's symbol and
remains standing today.

right
Designed by Willy Walter, the
"Radiant Structure" of the Swiss
Pavilion was composed of 370
tons of steel and aluminum and
was meant to represent the shape
of a tree. At night, the Swiss Pavilion glowed with 35,000 lights
in its filigreed metal facade.

left
Called the "World of Laughter," the Japanese Gas Industry Pavilion was intended to evoke a laughing man. It was designed by Ohbayashi-Gumi, Ltd.

opposite, left
Designed by Kiyonori Kikutake, the 417-foot-tall Expo Tower had an observation platform and wireless relay station.

opposite, right
Interior of the Expo Tower.

following spread, left
In the Textile Pavilion, "Innovations in Art" presented nude mannequins with Afros.

following spread, right
Made of sixteen vinyl tubes, the Fuji Pavilion was the world's largest pneumatic structure. It was designed by Yutaka Murata. In front of the Fuji Pavilion lie the canvas tents of the Japanese Automobile Manufacturers Association Pavilion.

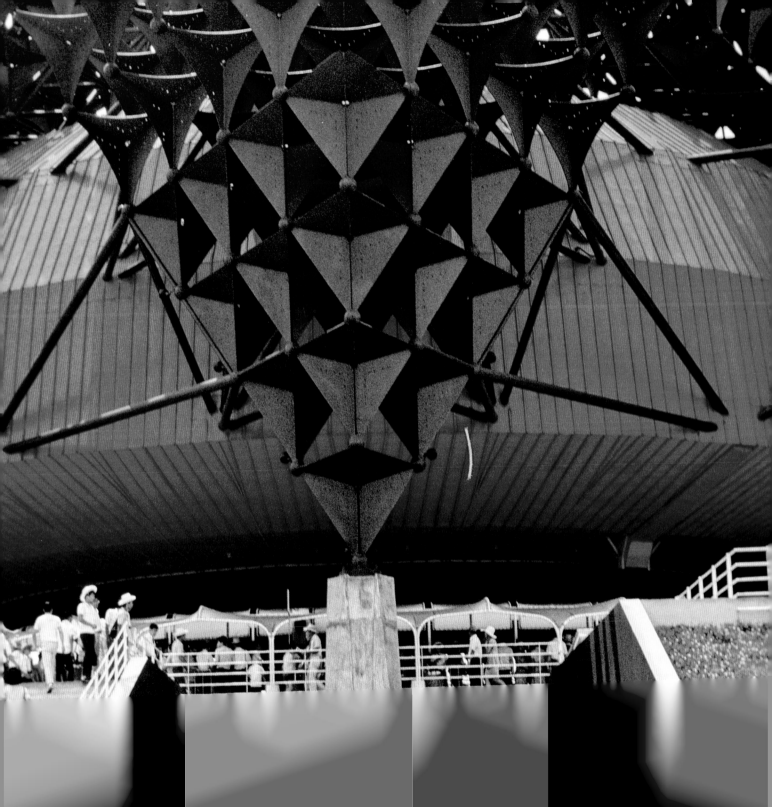

previous spread, left and right
At Kisho Kurokawa's Toshiba IHI Pavilion, prefabricated tetra-units supported the 180-foot-tall tower. The Toshiba IHI Pavilion was a giant space frame composed of 1,476 tetrahedron-shaped metal units. A red dome called the Global Vision Theater was suspended from the frame.

opposite and left
Designed for the Takara Group by Kurokawa, the Beautillion was composed of steel pipes and capsules. It was assembled on site in less than a week. At the Beautillion, the theme was the "Joy of Being Beautiful."

opposite
The 260-ton roof of the Australian Pavilion hung from a cantilevered support tower. Resembling a giant wave, the cantilevered support was inspired by Japanese woodcuts. The Australian architect James MacCormick designed the pavilion.

above
Inside the United States Pavilion, astronauts "floated" near their capsule.

left
At night, the Textile Pavilion was lit, exposing its structural system.

opposite
Inside the Tower of the Sun, the "Tree of Life" told the story of the evolution of man. Four escalators carried visitors past three hundred models of simple-celled creatures, birds, reptiles, fish, apes, and man.

above
Kenzo Tange designed the master plan as well as the superstructure of the main welcome pavilion with the Tower of the Sun. The tower had three faces: the "Black Sun," the "Golden Sun," and an unnamed face directed toward the main gate.

left
Called "The World of Laughter," the Japanese Gas Industry Pavilion was intended to evoke a laughing man.

above
Designed for Nippon Telephone, the Telecommunications Pavilion featured stretched yellow canvas. Inside, visitors were subjected to the crying of two hundred babies in a display about early human communication.

right
Beneath the Suntory Pavilion, visitors traveled on moving sidewalks inside tubes. Constructed of concrete, the pavilion was designed to resemble the traditional bamboo vessel for drinking sake.

Technical adventures into future living

■ The "Ultrasonic Bath" of the future for an effective preservation of health and beauty.
■ The "Flower Kitchen" with a total control system, making future cooking and eating a pleasure.

■ The "Home Information System", an electronic experiment in total comunication.
■ The "Health Capsule", a private world for complete physical and psychological relaxation.

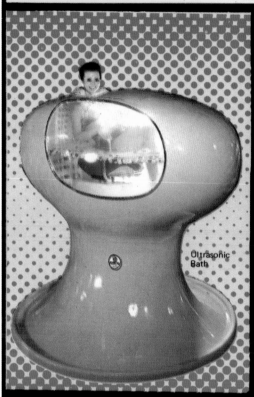

Ultrasonic Bath

Home Information System

Health Capsule

Flower Kitchen

EXPO'70 **SANYO**

above
For the kitchen of the modern home, the Sanyo Company provided information, a health capsule, and bath modules.

right
Elevated moving walkways carried visitors past the cantilevered arm of the Australian Pavilion.

opposite
With "the blissful hot water," the robotic washing machine cleansed with "ultrasonic bubbles."

1974-2002

IN THE LAST QUARTER of the twentieth century, world's fairs lost much of their glamour. Expositions increasingly lost money, and fewer countries and municipalities were willing to take on the financial burden of hosting elaborate fairs. Expos and world's fairs continued, but they became more issue-specific, and less international, universal, or futuristic in their character. They lacked the luster and exhilaration of earlier fairs.

With the noble aims of energy conservation and harnessing renewable resources, the Knoxville World's Fair of 1982 was titled "Energy Turns the World," but planning for the fair was disorganized. As the fair was being planned in the late 1970s, energy and the oil crisis were hot topics, but by 1982 energy conservation was no longer as popular a subject. Despite promises of financial success by organizers, the fair created $57 million in debt for the city. Three years later, the fair organizers gave refunds to more than twenty-seven hundred tourists for shabby or nonexistent accommodations when visiting Knoxville. The fair symbol, called the Sunsphere, was an uninspired sphere in reflective glass atop a glorified elevator shaft.

In 1984 New Orleans hosted the Louisiana World Exposition as a way to revitalize a run-down part of town. The theme was "World of Rivers: Freshwater as a Source for Life" and featured bare-breasted mermaid sculptures and a half-mile-long Wonderwall, a postmodern-style creation designed by Charles Moore and William Turnball, with urns, towers, columns, busts, pediments, and animal sculptures. The Wonderwall and the exposition failed to generate the same degree of delight and excitement of previous fairs and lost $157 million. In an ignominious ending, the marketing director of the fair was sentenced to jail for mail fraud because he illegally sold fair souvenirs through the mail.

The 1986 Vancouver World's Fair proved to be more successful. It was instrumental in developing the British Columbian city and attracted many immigrants to this booming town. The fairgrounds were an assemblage of dull, steel-framed, tented buildings. The last fair to be held in North America, it attracted almost twenty-two million visitors, less than half of Montreal's Expo '67 but double the number who attended the Knoxville World's Fair.

Held in the same year as the Olympics in Barcelona, the 1992 Seville World's Fair was part of Spain's year-long commemoration of the five hundredth anniversary of Columbus's voyage. The Spanish government spent more than $10 billion in improvements for infrastructure, including Santiago Calatrava's breathtaking Alamillo Bridge. The fair itself featured 110 country exhibits and sixty-three pavilions, including Tadao Ando's elegant Japanese Pavilion, the largest wood building in the world. Chile contributed an event, rather than a fair building, by towing an iceberg from Antarctica to the fair to create awareness of the delicate ecology of the planet. Other architects who contributed works included Jean Nouvel, Arata Isozaki, and Norman Foster.

Expo '93 in Taejon, Korea, was the first exposition to be held in a developing country. Although only three months long, it signaled the emergence of Korea as a leading scientific and technological leader.

To celebrate the five hundredth anniversary of Vasco da Gama's discovery of the sea route to India, Lisbon held an exposition in 1998, themed "The Oceans: A Heritage for the Future." The Oriente Station, a transportation hub in northeast Lisbon, deftly wove together various modes of transportation and served as the primary transportation connection for fairgoers. Designed by Santiago Calatrava, the Oriente Station was part of a massive effort to revitalize a derelict industrial area of Lisbon. The stunning roof of the Oriente Station employs a tree motif with columns and a roof canopy. Though not as popular as Vancouver's fair, the Lisbon exposition had more than 146 countries participating—one of the largest representations of nations in world's fair history.

Departing from tradition, Expo 2000 in Hanover, Germany, was the first world exposition to use existing buildings. Focused on "Humankind, Nature and Technology," the exposition presented solutions for the environmental problems of the twenty-first century, rather than general advances in technology or science. To examine how technology and nature can coexist, the Dutch architecture firm MVRDV designed a stunning pavilion of stacked landscapes. In this pavilion, nature and mankind were able to occupy the same space in an entirely new way.

At the 2002 Swiss National Exposition, the New York–based architects Diller + Scofidio presented a radically new pavilion with the Blur Building. A media pavilion at the base of Lake Neuchâtel, the Blur Building was formed by fine mists of water from the lake, shot through 31,500 nozzles, creating an artificial cloud around the pavilion structure. Its form continuously shifted. The pavilion structure was based on Buckminster Fuller's work, but it was unlike anything Fuller could have imagined.

Expositions are recovering their early glory as incubators of innovative design and technologies. Shanghai promises to host a spectacular fair in 2010, and many countries are preparing bids for the 2012 world's fair. The future holds much promise for world's fairs, as more countries are vying for expositions.

previous spread
At the Alamillo Bridge in Seville, Santiago Calatrava angled a pylon at fifty-eight degrees and connected the pylon to the bridge by cables, completely supporting the bridge from a single pylon.

above
The Japanese Pavilion for the 1992 Seville World's Fair, designed by Tadao Ando, used a traditional wood-slatted construction for the facade.

above
For the Kuwait Pavilion for the 1992 Seville World's Fair, Santiago Calatrava designed a moving roof system that resembles the fronds of a palm tree.

right
A tower from the 1993 exposition in Korea.

left
For the Oriente Station in Lisbon, Santiago Calatrava employed an innovative roof structure.

below
For Swiss Expo 2002, Diller Scofidio + Renfro constructed the Blur Building, a media pavilion at the base of Lake Neuchâtel. Fine mists of water from Lake Neuchâtel were shot through 31,500 nozzles, creating an artificial cloud around the pavilion structure.

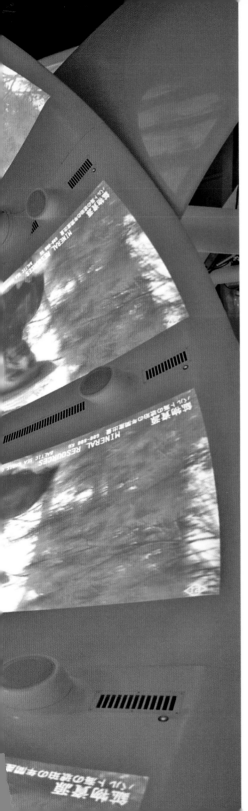

AICHI 2005

THE SECOND WORLD'S FAIR held in Japan, Expo 2005 focused on technology and how to address the environmental problems of the twenty-first century. The theme was "Nature's Wisdom," and corporate and national pavilions used renewable and recycled building materials, solar and wind power, and alternative fuel vehicles. Garbage receptacles around the fairground included twelve different recycling containers, and full-time recycling guides stood by to help fairgoers sort their recyclables. Groundbreaking technologies promised new modes of transportation, personal robots, and other fantastical conveniences. According to fair architect Yutaka Hikosaka, "The 150-year history of world expositions is a history of revolutions…. The Aichi Expo is being held at a time of environmental revolution, and explores ways to restore the links between humankind and nature."

Among the fair's novel technologies were the Linimo Line, a newly built, elevated, magnetic levitating subway link; Toyota's I-Unit, an electric-powered personal mobility device; and Japan Railway's Mag-Lev super bullet train, capable of attaining 360 mph. In keeping with the expo's environmental focus, fuel cell–powered unmanned Intelligent Multi-Mode Transit System buses shuttled visitors around the expo grounds.

Perhaps because of Japan's aging society and low birth rate, personal care and companion robots were a common feature throughout the fair. NEC's cute gnome-like PaPeRo child companion robots communicated with children in several languages and also had built-in video cameras for busy parents to monitor their children. A plush seal robot, meant to comfort the elderly and the sick, responded to human touch with wriggling body movements and blinking eyes. Such robots were contemporary versions of the Westinghouse Moto-Man from the 1939 World's Fair.

Grand pavilions, comparable to those of yesterday's fairs, reappeared at Aichi, but corporations, rather than nations, sponsored the more elaborate pavilions. A cascading waterfall divided the Hitachi Pavilion, reminiscent of the water effect at the 1939 Italian Pavilion. A gently curving ramp encircled the Toyota Pavilion. The circular building, made of reusable steel scaffolding and laminated paper, evoked Albert Kahn's General Motors Pavilion of 1939.

National pavilions were mostly modular, hangarlike structures with embellished facades. Inventive design was reserved for the interiors. With ramps and twisting trees in muted greens, China's display was both traditional and modern. Multiple video screens illustrated the technical and economic prowess of the "New China," as well as its recent environmental efforts. In a novel approach, Lithuania presented a white spiral display, resembling a DNA strand. Projected onto this spiral strand were Lithuanian television shows and interviews with citizens.

In a fair hosted by a non-Western country, the roster of countries participating was broader than that of recent expos and included even Iran and Cuba. As at most international expositions, there was a sense that the countries of the world could work together in harmony and peace, but the metal detectors and x-ray machines at the entrance to the U.S. Pavilion belied this sentiment and reminded visitors of the sober reality of world politics.

previous spread
In Lithuania's first appearance at a world's fair, it presented a spiral model resembling a strand of DNA. Video projections onto this spiral strand highlighted "the progress of civilization and culture."

below
A new super-conducting linear train capable of traveling at 360 miles per hour—the fastest manned rail vehicle in history—premiered at the Japanese Railway Pavilion. By watching a three-dimensional IMAX movie, visitors could virtually experience a journey at this previously unobtainable ground speed.

right
Bamboo covered the Japanese Pavilion to help control the heat of the sun. The roof of the Japanese Pavilion was made using photocatalytic tiles, and water was sprinkled on the roof to create a cooling effect. The pavilion design allowed visitors to experience the latest environmental technologies and materials.

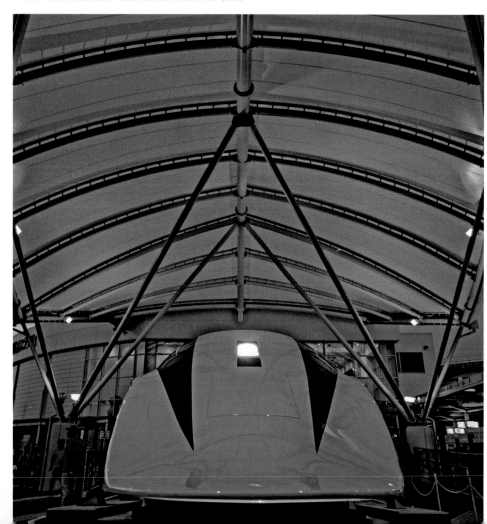

Built with removable and reusable steel couplings and a laminated paper façade, the Toyota Pavilion featured a ramp that evoked the 1939 General Motors Highways and Horizons Pavilion designed by Albert Kahn.

At the Robot Station, "Actroid," the robot hostess, provided information in four languages while dressed in a miniskirt and white plastic boots.

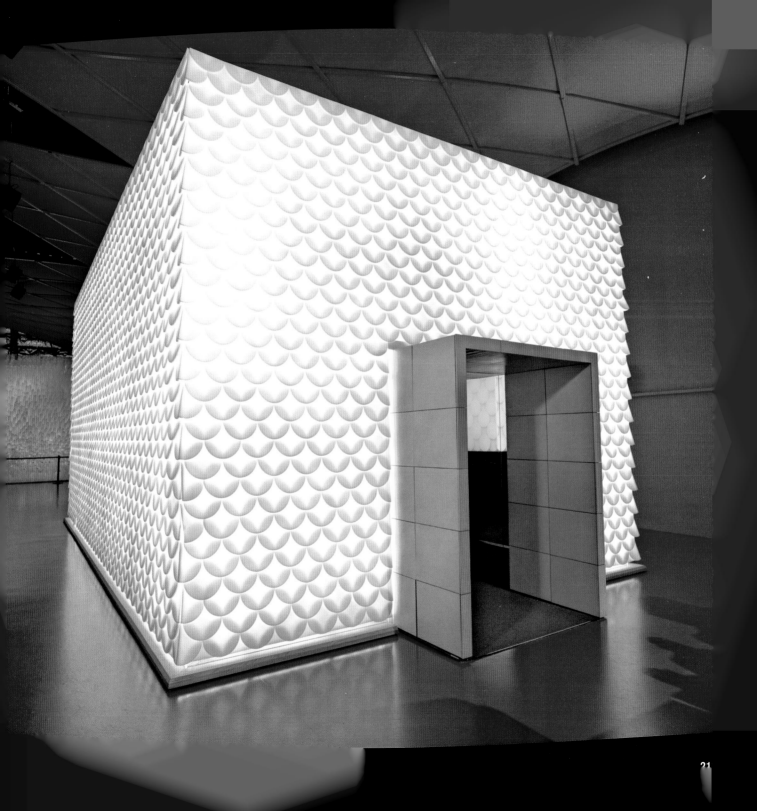

previous spread, left
The theme of the Chinese Pavilion was "Nature, City, Harmony—Art of Life."

previous spread, right
In the French Pavilion, Louis Vuitton presented a structure made of four thousand sea salt plates to symbolize sustainable development.

left
Nedo Robot Pavilion.

left
Shaped like a leaf, the Toyota I-Unit was a new type of "personal mobility" that aimed to give consumers freedom of movement as well as harmony with nature.

below
A demonstration of the Toyota I-Unit highlighted its ability to transform from a personal transport device—moving a person in an upright position—to stretch out into a highway-worthy vehicle. Built-in sensors helped the I-Unit avoid accidents.

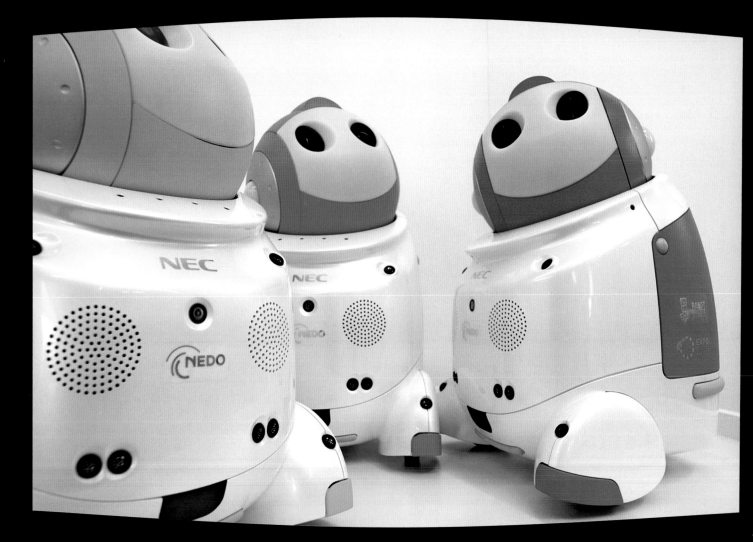

above
The NEC "PaPeRo" companion robots featured voice capabilities and built-in video cameras to monitor children, enabling busy parents to focus on other tasks.

opposite
In the Japanese Pavilion, large screens showed the changing environmental conditions of the planet.

looking to the future: world's fairs 1933–1980s

STEPHEN VAN DYK

SINCE THEIR INCEPTION IN THE MID-NINE-TEENTH CENTURY, world expositions have served in many roles as arenas of world commerce, as forums promoting advances in science and building construction showing the latest inventions, and as displays of raw materials and industry. World's fairs were also opportunities for expressions of nationalism, to see and learn about exotic peoples and cultures, for showcases of architectural design, and for county fair–like amusement parks. At the same time, world's fairs were the forerunners of modern museums, international trade shows, and global organizations concerned with world peace, economics, health, ecology, and the betterment of humankind.

Though fairs were frequently scheduled to celebrate the anniversary of a historic event (i.e., the four hundred years since the discovery of America at the World's Columbian Exposition in Chicago in 1893), they featured the latest achievements in science and technology and were vehicles for displaying futur-

istic ideas and inventions and for speculations about life in the future. Dave Walter's book *Today Then* includes seventy-four predictions of what life would be like one hundred years into the future as presented at the 1893 Chicago fair by "America's Best Minds." It was speculated that aluminum would be the metal of the future, postage would be reduced to one cent, electrical power would be universal and every home would have a telephone, trains would run one hundred miles per hour, and men would grow "wiser, better, and purer."

a home of their own

Fairs in the twentieth century continued to be forums for futuristic trends and for promoting the idea that progress through man's achievements would lead to a better life and ultimately world unity and peace. President William McKinley noted at the 1901 Pan-American Exposition in Buffalo that fairs "are the time-keepers of progress . . . they record the world's achievements." The "A Century of Prog-

ress" Exposition of 1933/34, commemorating Chicago's centennial, promoted this ideal that modern advancements in science and technology were the avenue to a hopeful and bright future—even in the midst of the nation's worst economic depression. The theme was "Science Finds, Industry Applies, Man Conforms." Visitors viewed displays of photo-electronic cell technology, modern incubators for infants, robots, a vertical parking lot, streamlined cars and trains, modern art deco pavilions, and airships. They could even enjoy a sky ride.

"Homes of Tomorrow," a group of twelve model houses on display in the Home and Industrial Arts area of the fair, was especially interesting because it provided a wide range of styles employing new construction methods and materials that were affordable and therefore accessible to a growing number of Americans seeking homes of their own. Featured were prefabricated units that used new building materials such as masonite, pressed stone called Rostone,

Armco-Ferro enamel, cypress, glass, and steel, as well as traditional brick and lumber. The latest labor-saving devices and modern conveniences such as central air-conditioning and an all-electric kitchen gave the visitor a preview of an actual future home. Keck & Keck's "House of Tomorrow," known as "America's first glass house," was a twelve-sided structure comprised of steel and glass. Unlike the other models it was not affordable to the average American, but it did serve as an example of Bauhaus-inspired design that would dominate commercial architecture in the U.S. in the decades that followed. In contrast, architect Howard Fisher exhibited a prefabricated, one story, all-steel house that sold for $4,000 by General Houses, Inc., who boasted that they could build "houses in an assembly-line method like Fords."

planning the city in the world of tomorrow

As American suburbs developed slowly in the 1930s—some actually incorporating the futuristic prefabs exhibited at Chicago in 1933/34—interest in the study of future urban and town planning grew. The 1939/40 fair in New York, with the theme "Building the World of Tomorrow," continued the World's Fair tradition of premiering new inventions—notably nylon stockings and the television set—while commemorating the 150th anniversary of George Washington's inauguration in New York. Like the Chicago fair, this exposition stressed that advances in science and industry were the key to building the future world. Ironically, the planners envisioned that the exposition would act as a venue for peaceful interaction among nations—even on the brink of World War II.

Several corporate-sponsored exhibits contributed to the theme of a better future through technology. Among them most notably were Westinghouse's time capsule, a display of model homes called the "Town of Tomorrow," Raymond Loewy's futuristic transport called "Rocketport," a General Motors exhibition titled "Futurama," and "The World of the Day After Tomorrow"—a series of displays designed by Donald Deskey for Bristol-Myers.

a notable cause

The idea of a better life and a more humane, peaceful world through achievements in science and technologies was again the theme at Expo '58 in Brussels. The planners of the fair were faced with the challenge of situating the exposition in a European location still recovering from the destruction of World War II and one that, during the cold war, essentially pitted the Soviet Union against the United States. To add to the drama, the focal point of the fair, symbolized by a large stainless-steel structure called the Atomium, was the atom that a little over a decade before had been used to destroy Hiroshima and Nagasaki. Expo '58, however, concentrated on the international study of pure science and the future peaceful uses of nuclear energy and the atom. Organizers were faced with the goal of fostering cooperation rather than competition among exhibitors (particularly among the superpowers), who were displaying positive uses of the atom in an interesting yet meaningful way to a lay audience concerned with nuclear fallout. Popular exhibits included interactive "electro-mechanical" hands, and guides were available to explain more technical exhibits along with a two-week-long show developed in conjunction with the 1958 Second International Geneva Conference on the Pacific Uses of Atomic Energy. The USSR exhibited atomic stations and submarines—perhaps more in a competitive spirit than the more benign U.S. Pavilion entitled the "American Way of Life." Overall the fair promoted a sense of techno-optimism, a greater understanding of nuclear energy, and increased cooperation among the scientific community, and to that end, this notable cause was truly successful.

new frontiers

Four years later, at the 1962 Century 21 Exposition in Seattle, Washington, increased competition between America and the Soviets concerned quality of life, ideological issues, and the new frontier of outer space. Within this environment of the yet-to-be-discovered world of outer space, however, forecasters envisioned future life on earth in 2001 filled with "space-age" inventions. These included the fully "push-button" home with au-

tomated cooking, cleaning, storage, and entertainment facilities; air-cushioned cars, trains, and supersonic airplanes; new processed and vitamin-enriched foods; home computers for record keeping, shopping, and bill paying; push button and cordless phones; men walking on the moon; and schools monitored by televisions.

A larger and highly commercial counterpart to the Seattle fair was held in New York in 1964/1965, on the brink of America's involvement in the Vietnam War. The theme of a better future through science and world cooperation was expressed through the exposition's optimistic themes: "Man's Achievements in an Expanding World," "A Millennium of Progress," "Peace through Understanding," and "It's a Small World." The fair explored new technological frontiers in the space age with displays of space capsules and rockets, the information age with IBM computers and electronic calculators, the atomic age with nuclear fusion, and a new consumer age with DuPont's "Wonderful World of Chemistry" display of plastic fabric and molded products. The fair was dominated by exhibitions sponsored by major American corporations ranging from insurance companies to automobile manufacturers. Disney had a significant presence at the fair, developing a number of audio-animatronics (motion figures) for the It's a Small World, Magic Skyway, and the Car-

ousel of Progress pavilions—some that would later be installed at Disney World, the theme park that would take the atmosphere of amusement away from world's fairs of the future.

changing roles

One of the last large international fairs was held in Montreal and known as Expo '67, commemorating Canada's centennial with the theme of "Man and His World." Though the fair focused more on an international rather than a commercial presence, it was similar to the recent New York fair in that it was situated within the core of the city, was an occasion for innovative architecture, and relied more on animation and film than on the display of objects as in previous fairs. The fair, however, raised interesting questions. In the "Man the Explorer" exhibition the issues of technology's effect on the environment were raised in a film in the section labeled "Is Man in Control?" Was it possible that perhaps science and technology were not the answer to a better life? Moshe Safdie's Habitat '67, an apartment complex consisting of a series of concrete modules stacked in unexpected patterns, addressed the question of whether such structures could provide modern and efficient urban housing as an alternative to the suburban single-family ranch-style house.

Audiovisual and film presentations were the dominant feature of the world's first major fair to be held in Asia in Osaka, Japan, in 1970. The theme was "Progress and Harmony for Mankind," and the fair featured innovative building structures such as Kenzo Tange's massive clear glass-roofed Festival Hall, and the large tent covering the U.S. and Fuji Group pavilions that employed air systems to support the structure. And yet, among these laser, film, and audio presentations housed in expansive contemporary structures, was a simple film in the Scandinavian Pavilion on pollution control in northern Europe—a changing role in looking into the future.

world's fairs of the future

There have been a number of small regional fairs since Osaka's Expo '70, including an Expo '74 in Spokane, Washington, that focused on the environment; an international energy fair in Knoxville, Tennessee, in 1982; the 1984 New Orleans exhibition investigating fresh water as a source of life; the 1985 Tsukuba, Japan, fair whose theme was "Science and Technology for Man at Home"; a look at highways at the Expo '86 in Vancouver; and "The Age of Discoveries" in Seville in 1992. What seems clear is that fairs after Expo '70 have been less expansive, located in smaller cities, and more focused on specific issues and themes. Their appeal has been significantly lessened in many cases by the very technologies and ideas that they originally promoted. New building construction methods, i.e., large-scale prefabricated structures, have been used to develop international convention centers that host trade fairs and conferences. Supersonic jets, high-speed cars, and trains, as well as interstate superhighway systems, are commonplace today, facilitating travel to cultural, educational, and recreational places and events that once made world's fairs a destination in themselves.

Electronic and communication devices that premiered at fairs now provide ubiquitous and instantaneous information on new products and technological advancements. Amusement sections that were once standard attractions at fairs have been replaced by theme parks, while museums have become the major venues for displays of natural sciences, inventions, and fine and decorative arts. At the same time, such events as the Olympics and such organizations as the United Nations are now the forums for nations to gather and seek solutions to world conflicts.

And yet, taking all of these facts into account, there seems to be a future for world's fairs even in our ever-shrinking world. Expositions are still great venues for the display of new architecture by some of the most talented designers of our time. How wonderful it would be if some of the monuments, parks, transportation systems, and buildings created for these events would live on to revitalize cities and regional areas. Future fairs planned in more remote sites could stimulate local economy through tourism. Technologies and ideas for the betterment of humankind should be presented as a global concern. But most important, expositions in the future should continue to concentrate on the ideal—by being arenas of discovery and education where issues such as world health, world peace, and improvement of the environment are the central focus and where the achievements of humankind are celebrated.

bibliography

Allwood, John. *Great Exhibitions*. London 1977.

Altick, Richard D. *The Shows of London*. Cambridge, Massachusetts 1978.

Appelbaum, Stanley, ed. *The New York World's Fair 1939/1940*. New York 1977.

Art and Power: Europe Under the Dictators, 1935–45. London 1995.

Auerbach, Jeffrey A. *The Great Exhibition of 1851: A Nation on Display*. New Haven 1999.

Baculo, A., S. Gallo, and M. Mangore. *Le grandi Esposizioni nel Mondo, 1851–1900*. Naples 1988.

Bannister, T. C. "Bogardus Revisited." *Journal of the Society of Architectural Historians*, nos. 15 and 16. 1956 and 1957.

Benjamin, W. "Grandville or the World Exhibitions." In *Baudelaire: A Lyrical Poet in the Era of High Capitalism*. London 1989.

Besset, M. *Gustave Eiffel*. Paris 1957.

Bogardus, James. *Cast Iron Buildings*. 1856.

Bolotin, Norman, and Christine Laing. *The World's Columbian Exhibition*. Chicago 2002.

Bosbach, Franz. *The Great Exhibition and Its Legacy*. Munich 2002.

Burton, Benedict L. *The Anthropology of World's Fairs*. 1983.

Chadwick, G. F. *The Works of Sir Joseph Paxton, 1803–1865*. London 1961.

Clasen, Wolfgang. *Expositions, Exhibits, Industrial and Trade Fairs*. New York 1968.

Coombs, Robert. "Norman Bel Geddes." *Perspecta*, no. 13/14. 1971.

Crary, Jonathan. *Techniques of the Observer: On Vision and Modernity in the 19th Century*. Cambridge, Massachusetts 1990.

Crouzet, Francois. *The Victorian Economy*. London 1982.

Cruz-Diez, José. "Chilean Pavilion Seville Expo." *Architectural Design* Jan.–Feb. 2003.

"Dawn of a New Day." *The New York World's Fair 1939/1940*. Exhibition catalogue. Flushing, New York: Queens Museum of Art, 1980.

De Jonge, Alex. *Dostoevsky and the Age of Intensity*. New York 1975.

Dernberg, Friedrich. *Aus der weissen Stadt*. Berlin 1893.

Drew, Philip. *Frei Otto: Form and Structure*. Boulder 1976.

Eisenbauten: Ihre Geschichte und Aesthetik. Esslingen 1907.

"Expo '70: East meets West." *Newsweek*. 9 March 1970.

Fay, C. R. *Palace of Industry, 1851*. Cambridge, England 1951.

Findling, John E. *Chicago's Great World's Fairs*. Manchester 1994.

Frank, Joseph. *Dostoevsky: The Stir of Liberation, 1860–1865*. Princeton 1986.

Friemert, Chup. *Die gläserne Arche: Kristallpalast London 1851 und 1854*. Munich 1984.

Fuller, R. Buckminster. *Nine Chains to the Moon*. New York 1938.

Gaillard, Marc. *Paris: Les expositions universelles de 1855 à 1937*. Paris 2003.

Gause, Jo Allen, ed. *Great Planned Communities*. Washington, D.C. 2002.

Gelernter, David. *1939: Lost World of Fair*. New York 1995.

Geddes, Patrick. *Industrial Exhibitions and Modern Progress*. 1887.

Geppert, Alexander C. T., Jean Coffey, and T. Lau. *International Exhibitions, 1851–1951: A Bibliography*. Florence 2000.

Giedion, Sigfried. *Bauen in Frankreich*. Leipzig 1928. Translated under the title *Building in France* (Santa Monica 1995).

———. *Zeit, Raum, Architektur*. Ravensburg 1965 (first 1958).

Gold, John R., and Margaret M. Gold. *Cities of Culture: Staging International Festivals and the Urban Agenda, 1951–2000*. Burlington, Vermont 1988.

Gräfe, Rainer. "Projektbereich Architektur. Geschichte des Konstruierens. Hängedächer des 19. Jahrhunderts." *arcus*, no. 2. 1985.

Greenhalgh, P. "Ephemeral Vistas: The Exhibitions Universelles." *Great Exhibitions and World's Fairs, 1851–1939*. Manchester 1987.

Gregg, Richard A. "Two Adams and Eva in the Crystal Palace: Dostoevsky, the Bible, and We." *Major Soviet Writers: Essays in Criticism*, edited by Edward J. Brown. London 1973.

Günschel, G. *Grosse Konstrukteure*, vol. 1. Berlin 1966.

Harrison, Helen A., ed. *Dawn of a New Day: The New York World's Fair, 1939/1940*. New York 1980.

Helmreich, Anne. "The Nation and the Garden. England and the World's Fairs at the Turn of the Century." *Art, Culture, and National Identity in Fin-de-Siècle Europe*, edited by M. Focos and S. L. Hirsh. Cambridge, England 2003.

Hilton, Suzanne. *Here Today and Gone Tomorrow: The Story of World's Fairs and Expositions*. Philadelphia 1978.

Holt, E. G., ed. *The Triumph of Art for the Public: The Emerging Role of Exhibitions and Critics*. Garden City 1979.

Hines, T. S. *Burnham of Chicago: Architect and Planner*. New York 1974.

Hobhouse, Christopher. *1851 and the Crystal Palace*. London 1937.

Hoffenberg, Peter H. *An Empire on Display: English, Indian, and Australian Exhibitions from the Crystal Palace to the Great War*. Berkeley 2001.

Hoffmann, H. *Deutschland in Paris*. Munich 1937.

Isay, R. *Panorama des expositions universelles*. Paris 1937.

Jordan, Hermann. *Die künstlerische Gestaltung von Eisenkonstruktionen*. 2 vols. Berlin 1913.

Keim, J. A. *La Tour Eiffel*. Paris 1950.

Kultermann, Udo. *Architecture and Revolution: The Visions of Boullée and Ledoux*. Budapest 2003.

———. "Ausstellungsarchitektur Brüssel." *Baukunst und Werkform*, no. 6. 1958.

———. *Der Schlüssel zur Architektur von heute*. Duesseldorf 1963.

———. *Kenzo Tange: Architecture and Urban Design*. Zurich 1970.

———. "Konstruktion, Architektur und das fehlende Atomium." *form*, no. 3. 1958.

———. *Visible Cities – Invisible Cities*. St. Louis 1988.

Kultermann, Udo, ed. *St. James Modern Masterpieces: The Best of Art, Architecture, Photography, and Design Since 1945*. Detroit 1997.

"L'Exposition de Philadelphia." *Gazette des architecture et du batiment*, no. 12. 1876.

Lampugnani, Vittorio. "Von der E 42 zur EUR." In *Das Bauwerk und die Stadt*, edited by Wolfgang Böhm. Vienna 1994.

Lebedev, J. S. *Architektur und Bionik*. Berlin 1983 (first published in Russian in 1977).

Lewis, Arnold. *An Early Encounter with Tomorrow*. Chicago 1997.

Lewis, Beth Irwin. *Art for All?* Princeton 2003.

Libera, Adalberto, and Mario De Renzi. *La facciata della Mostra delle Rivoluzione Fascista*. Rome 1932.

Lingeri, P., G. Terragni, and C. Cattaneo. *Progetto per il Palazzo dei Congressi all' E 42*. Rome 1938.

Linn, James Weber. Introduction to *A Century of Progress Exposition Chicago, 1933*. Chicago 1933.

Lockman, Carol Ressler. *Utopian Visions and World's Fairs*. Symposium at the Hagley Library and Museum, Wilmington, Delaware, 15 April 2005.

Luckhurst, K. W. *The Story of Exhibitions*. London 1951.

Maass, John. "The Glorious Enterprise." *The Centennial Exhibition of 1876 and A. J. Schwarzmann, Architect-in-chief*. New York 1973.

Malamud, Carl. *A World's Fair for the Global Village*. Cambridge, Massachusetts 1997.

Mandell, Richard D. *Paris 1900*. Toronto 1967.

Markham, V. *Paxton and the Bachelor Duke*. London 1935.

Mattie, Erik. *World's Fairs*. Princeton 1998.

McHale, J. *R. Buckminster Fuller*. New York 1962.

Meyer-Bohe, W. *Vorfertigung: Handbuch des industriellen Bauens*. Essen 1964.

Mumford, Lewis. *Architecture*. Chicago 1926.

———. *The Culture of Cities*. New York 1938.

———. *From the Ground Up*. New York 1947.

———. *Roots of Contemporary American Architecture*. New York 1952.

———. *Sticks and Stones*. New York 1924.

Neuburg, Hans. *Conception of International Exhibitions*. Zurich 1969.

Noto, Cosimo. *The Ideal City*. New York 1903.

Nye, David E. *Electrifying America: Social Meanings of a New Technology; 1880–1940*. Cambridge, Massachusetts 1990.

Otto, Frei. *Das hängende Dach*. Berlin 1954.

Peer, S. *Vorfertigung auf der Baustelle*. Cologne 1964.

Pelli, Cesar. "Joseph Paxton's Crystal Palace." *a+u: architecture and urbanism*, no. 2. 1980.

Pevsner, N. *High Victorian Design: A Study of the Exhibits of 1851*. London 1957.

Plato, Alice von. *Präsentierte Geschichte: Ausstellungskultur und Massenpublikum im Frankreich des 19. Jahrhunderts*. Frankfurt 2001.

Poirier, R. *Des Foires, des peuples, des expositions*. Paris 1958.

Purbrick, Louise. *The Great Exhibition of 1851*. Manchester 2001.

Robbe, Deborah. *Expositions and Trade Shows*. New York 2000.

Roland, C. "Frei Otto." *Spannweiten*. Berlin 1965.

Rolt, L. T. C. *George and Robert Stephenson*. London 1960.

———. *Isambard Kingdom Brunel*. London 1957.

Rydell, Robert W. *All the World's a Fair*. Chicago 1984.

Rydell, Robert W., John E. Findling, and Kimberly D. Pelle. *Fair America: World's Fairs in the United States*. Washington, D.C. 2000.

Safdie, Moshe. *Beyond Habitat*. Cambridge, Massachusetts 1970.

———. "Habitat at 25." *Architectural Record*, July 1992.

Samuels, E., ed. *Henry Adams*. New York 1983.

Shaw, Marian. *World's Fair Notes: A Woman Journalist Views Chicago's 1893 Columbian Exhibition*. Chicago 1992.

Sigel, Paul. *Deutsche Pavillons auf Weltausstellungen*. Berlin 2000.

Tafuri, Manfredo, and Francesco Dal Co. *Architettura Contemporanea*. Milan 1976.

Tamir, M. *Les expositions internationales a travers les ages*. Paris 1939.

Tilly, Richard. "Globalisierung aus historischer Sicht und das Lernen aus der Geschichte." *Kölner Vorträge zur Sozial- und Wirtschaftsgeschichte*, no. 41. Cologne 1999.

Tompkins, Calvin. "Man and Whose World?" *The New Yorker*. 26 August 1967.

Tzonis, Alexander. *Santiago Calatrava: The Poetics of Movement*. New York 1999.

———. *Memory and Invention*. London 1992.

Tzonis, Alexander, and Liane Lefaivre. *Architektur in Europa seit 1968*. Frankfurt 1992.

Upjohn, E. M. "Buffington and the Skyscraper." *The Art Bulletin*, no. 17. 1935.

Velarde, Giles. *Designing Exhibitions*. Burlington 2001.

Verger, Pierre. *Exposition '37: 60 photographies*. Paris 1937.

Veronesi, G. *Difficolta politiche dell' architettura in Italia, 1920–1940*. Milan 1953.

Wachsmann, Konrad. "Machine Energy: The Technique of Our Time." *Building for Modern Man*, edited by Thomas H. Creighton. Princeton 1949 .

———. *Wendepunkt im Bauen*. Wiesbaden 1949.

Wise, Michael Z. "Walking Mussolini's Fascist Utopia." *The New York Times*, 11 July 1999.

Wörner, Walter. *Vergnügung ung Belehrung: Volkskultur auf den Weltausstellungen, 1851–1900*. Muenster 1999.

Zim, Larry, Mel Lerner, and Herbert Rolfes. *The World of Tomorrow: The 1939 New York World's Fair*. New York 1988.

Zukowsky, John, ed. *Chicago Architecture and Design, 1923–1993*. Munich 1993.

credits